BEE HIVE
PRODUCT
BIBLE

BEE HIVE PRODUCT BIBLE

ROYDEN BROWN

AVERY PUBLISHING GROUP INC.

Garden City Park, New York

The diet and health procedures in this book are based on the personal experiences and research of the author. Because each person and situation are unique, the publisher urges the reader to check with a qualified health professional before using any procedure where there is any question as to its appropriateness.

The publisher does not advocate the use of any particular diet program but believes that the information presented in this book should be available to the public.

Because there is always some risk involved, the author and publisher are not responsible for any adverse effects or consequences resulting from the use of any of the suggestions, preparations, or procedures in this book. Please do not use the book if you are unwilling to assume the risk. Feel free to consult a physician or other qualified health professional. It is a sign of wisdom, not cowardice, to seek a second or third opinion.

Cover design: Rudy Shur and Janine Eisner-Wall
Artist: Tom Szumouki
Editor: Nikki Antol
In-House Editor: Elaine Will Sparber
Typesetter: Bonnie Freid
Printer: Paragon Press, Honesdale, Pennsylvania

Library of Congress Cataloging-in-Publication Data

Brown, Royden.
    [Bee hive product Bible]
    Royden Brown's Bee hive product Bible / Royden Brown.
        p. cm.
    Includes bibliographical references and index.
    ISBN 0-89529-521-0
    1. Bee products—Health aspects. I. Title. II. Title: Bee hive
product Bible.
RA784.B725 1993
615'.36—dc20   93-3222
                                                      CIP

Printed in the United States of America.

10 9 8 7 6 5 4 3 2 1

CONTENTS

*Unique among all God's creatures,
only the honeybee improves the environment
and preys not on any other species.*

I fondly dedicate *Royden Brown's Bee Hive Product Bible* to the humans who share the Earth with the quite remarkable honeybee. This book is a joyous celebration of the life of *Apis mellifera,* the little critter who works so hard to provide mankind with the mysterious and powerful products of the beehive.

FOREWORD

Since antiquity, man has been a consumer of bee products as dietary supplements. Down through the ages, he has unfailingly expressed the conviction that bee products improve health, vigor, and vitality. While such historical practices and empirical observations cannot medically be accepted as proof of the great benefits of beehive products, these reports have nonetheless been responsible for attracting a diverse and persistent scientific community to the study of the products of the beehive. The facts and analyses deduced from worldwide research consistently show beneficial effects when bee products are ingested by man. The data presented in this book have been culled and compiled from highly respected sources. Included are exhaustive analyses of the chemical composition and function of the various elements found in bee products. Data from archeological studies of pollen-shell markings and genetics reflect channels of population and food migration as well as historical weather patterns.

From my perspective as a physician, I have reviewed the scientific inquiries and have considered the clinical and nutritional findings on the products of the bee published throughout the world by respected authorities. These studies invariably show bee products to possess a high nutritive value. The products of the beehive are composed of identifiable and measurable metabolically active substances consisting of variable concentrations of protein and free amino acids plus a balanced array of biologically active substrates including hormones, enzymes, coenzymes, vitamins, minerals, trace elements, and sterols.

The stimulus to the increased strength and endurance effects of bee products in humans appears to stem from the specific actions and high concentration of live enzymes, which provide energy for attaching, splitting, transferring, and transporting biochemical elements; carotenoids, which are highly reactive energy sources that bind and hold elements together; lipids and phospholipids; and necessary nutrients, such as vitamin C and the essential amino acids lysine and valine.

The anti-infective properties of propolis and royal jelly against colds, open wounds, and chronic prostatitis have been shown to result from the antimicrobial activity of specific agents in bee products. These agents have been identified and shown in tests to be effective against bacteria and fungi. The nutritive elements of the beehive products as well as the numerous other characteristics and attributes are covered in the text of this book.

To provide testimony to the profound effects the products of the beehive exert on the human body, Royden Brown has accessed the enormous body of literature produced by the scientific community of nations around the globe and investigated masses of data showing the qualitative and quantitative provable attributes of bee products. He has categorized and set forth herein the personal experiences of scores of professional scientists, medical specialists, nutritionists, athletes, physical-fitness experts, and lay-witness consumers of bee products.

This book should prove extremely helpful and informative to laypersons and professionals alike. The author has extracted, synthesized, and summarized worldwide investigative findings in terms free of scientific jargon and presents the text entertainingly intertwined with personal experiences and collected knowledge.

Herbert B. Avery, M.D.
Los Angeles, California

PREFACE

The products of the beehive have been used as both food and medicine for millennia. As far back as 2735 B.C., the Chinese emperor Shen Nung compiled a vast medical encyclopedia, still authoritative today, that features the gifts of the bees. As recently as A.D. 1991, Columbia University published a study on the cancer-fighting properties of one bee-made product, propolis. The nutritive value of hive products has been established so many times in the laboratories of the world that it cannot be disputed.

In this book, you'll learn about many of the important research sources I used to formulate my beliefs and theories. You'll also find out what today's medical detectives and scientists have discovered about the products of the beehive. In effect, I've done your homework for you. Now make your own judgment. Reach your own conclusions.

All health authorities agree diet and lifestyle are enormously important in keeping us well. Medical science says diet and lifestyle are key components for optimizing good health, for staying younger longer, for enjoying quality time well into our golden years. Extending our natural life span past the Biblical three-score years and ten is not only possible but within our grasp.

I live the Apiarian Lifestyle, described in Chapter 8. I know it will work for you, too. Your body—and every cell within it—requires specific nutrients to keep it young, healthy, active, and attractive. The products of the beehive provide these nutrients, and a whole lot more, as you will see.

In the form of some direct quotes from translated scientific studies, here's a small sample of what you'll learn about the various products of the beehive:

Bee pollen is a complete food. The optimum of vigor and resistance to poor health and disease was obtained by adding twenty percent bee pollen to food. Bee pollen is rich in rare and precious nutritive compounds. It works in a deep and lasting fashion.

Royal Society of Naturalists
of Belgium and France

Studies have shown that subjects can live indefinitely on a diet of bee pollen and water. Chemical analyses show quality bee pollen contains every nutrient necessary to life—and something more, some "magic" the bee puts in. Bee pollen cannot be manufactured in a laboratory. This very complex substance contains factors science has not yet been able to identify, cannot synthesize. Some authorities believe these mysterious factors account for the remarkable health-promoting attributes of bee pollen.

Propolis has more and more drawn attention as a stimulator of the immunologic reaction. In the Department of Microbiology of the Kazan Institute, the favorable impact of propolis on immunogenesis has been established.

Kazan Institute, USSR

Propolis provides a documented boost to the immune system. Often called Russian penicillin, this beehive product is the most powerful antibiotic in Nature. It is also antiseptic, antifungal, antibacterial, and antimicrobial. There are no manufactured drugs that fight a virus, but propolis has antiviral properties.

Royal jelly is a powerful agent which starts up and revives the functions of cells and glands. Royal jelly preserves life and strength, delays the aging process, retains youthful freshness of body and mind.

H. W. Schmidt, M.D.
German Medical Association

Royal jelly's legendary promise of a longer life span and extension of youthful powers, appearance, and well-being far into old age has been documented clinically many times.

In this book, I will give you an in-depth review of the scientific and clinical documentation that provides incontrovertible proof of the benefits the products of the beehive can provide. You'll even meet a few people whose lives bear witness to the health-promoting powers of the bee's gifts.

I will also give you a rare peek into the society of the beehive, as well as a look at the legends and lore surrounding these hard-working little creatures. I know some people don't care for bees, shudder at the sight of those fuzzy little critters innocently sipping nectar from a flower, shoo them away, fear being stung. Understandable. A sting hurts. It's small consolation knowing the bee dies after using her stinger.

One of the studies I ran across during my research showed a consumer won't buy a jar of honey that carries a picture of a bee. This explains why the containers of honey in your supermarket don't show a real honeybee, although a few carry a stylized cartoon of one. Some containers of honey are shaped like a honey bear, presumably because bears are notoriously fond of honey and are thought of as cute and cuddly. I'd rather face a bee than a bear any day. I am very fond of bees. I have two beehives behind my garage and tend them myself.

My company's logo is a silhouette of a bee. The outline of the bee is true to life. However, we did depart from reality in one instance. Our bee carries a tiny basket in one of her "hands." Because we are bee-pollen harvesters, this basket represents the bee's pollen baskets, which are actually scooped-out depressions on the rear legs.

In an effort to win your understanding and admiration for

the honeybee, I will open this book with the historical perspective. In the Introduction, I will give you an overview of my own history with the bee. Then, in Chapter 1, I will tell you all about the bee, beehive society, and bee lore, and in Chapter 2, I will discuss beekeeping past and present. The beehive products will be discussed next. In Chapter 3, you'll learn all about bee pollen. In Chapter 4, you'll learn about propolis. Chapter 5 will be devoted to royal jelly. And honey will be the focus of Chapter 6. Using the beehive products with animals—horses, dogs, and cats—will be the subject of Chapter 7. And in Chapter 8, I'll describe the Apiarian Lifestyle, which is my lifestyle.

I would like this book to be an introduction to the beehive products. But even more, I'd like it to be a guide to healthy living. With a store of beehive products and a good attitude and healthy habits, a long and robust life follows naturally. I'm planning on living the millennium. How about you?

Royden Brown

Introduction

If you usually skip over the introduction of a book, please don't pass this one by. If you are skeptical of all the benefits claimed for the products of the beehive, you are in the same frame of mind as I once was. Are you hard to convince? So am I. I required scientifically and medically documented proof of the efficacy of the bee's products. I got it. Now I'm passing it on to you.

This book is the culmination of a personal quest that spans the last twenty years. I wrote this book because I honestly and sincerely believe the products of the beehive are perfect foods for humankind, God-given miracle foods, foods that both nourish and heal.

To understand why I am so urgently compelled to spread the good news about the bee's gifts to mankind, let me explain just how I came to feel such enthusiasm for all the beehive products.

My personal fascination with the bee and her products originated in England in the 1940s. Before the American entry into World War II, I joined the Royal Canadian Air Force as a fighter pilot. I was based in London and flying with the British Royal Air Force when a fellow pilot introduced me to bee pollen in the officers' mess. His description of the benefits of the golden grains of bee pollen was overenthusiastic, to say the least.

When I laughed at my friend, he gave me an article to read that had appeared in the London *Times*. This article extolled the properties of bee pollen, claiming bee pollen was a miracle food, a substance that would, given time, cure everything. "That's ridiculous," I said. I couldn't believe such a simple, little bee food could possibly be the miraculous substance the article claimed it to be. I promptly forgot all about it. I had a lot more on my mind than bees. The Blitz was on, and the war was keeping me pretty busy.

By the 1950s, I was back in the States, married, the father of two, and associated with Brighton State Bank in Brighton, Colorado. I ran across some articles on bee pollen telling about interesting studies that seemed to bear out the statements my fellow RAF pilot had made fifteen years before. I still wasn't convinced, mind you. I promptly forgot about bee pollen again.

Sometime in the 1960s, I read about bee pollen once more. Then I ran across several additional references to the products of the beehive, notably bee pollen. These articles piqued my curiosity anew. At this point, I determined to find out for myself the true nutritional value of bee pollen. I decided to investigate this "miracle from the beehive," a substance many people were calling the only perfect food on Earth.

By now, my family and I had relocated to Arizona. I started my research at the Phoenix Public Library, but there wasn't much on file about bee pollen back then. I ended up at the Arizona State University libraries. They proved to be a gold mine. I proceeded to read every article, every book, every study, every bit of information, I could find about bee pollen. By the time I was finished reading all that material, I had reached the inescapable conclusion that those articles I had seen over the years were not only true but may have actually *under*stated the facts.

I decided to try bee pollen on myself and my family. I purchased a package of bee-pollen tablets in a local health-food store. They were hard and dry, not very tasty, but I insisted the whole family partake. I didn't know it at the time, but those compressed tablets were made with imported bee pollen. We took the tablets regularly. It did seem we all stayed pretty healthy, but we were following a generally healthy lifestyle in the first place.

I realized this personal experiment with bee pollen was hardly conclusive. Still, I carried on with my little family study. When I learned the bee-pollen tablets we were taking were made from a single imported pollen source, I realized why they were so unappetizing. They were old and stale. Based on the studies I had read, I knew I needed to find an active bee-pollen product, one composed of pollen from a variety of floral sources and kept beehive fresh by deep freezing. My patriotism demanded I buy American.

I began searching for fresh bee pollen. Local Arizona bee-keepers weren't much interested in harvesting bee pollen for me, although I did buy fresh raw honey from one of them. I finally found a friendly California beekeeper who agreed to sell me bee pollen that was multicolored, evidence his bees gathered it from many pollen sources. In addition, he froze his bee pollen as soon as he took it from the beehive. This was the beehive-fresh pollen I wanted. What a difference! Those fresh granules actually tasted good. This beekeeper packaged his multifloral bee pollen for me in 30-pound buckets. I purchased probably about 210 pounds per year for many years.

By the early 1970s, it became apparent *something* was making a real difference in our household. Year after year, both of my children received awards for perfect attendance at school. Not one of us was ever sick, not even a sniffle or bout with the flu. We didn't have a family doctor; we had no need for one.

I was convinced. It simply had to be the bee pollen keeping us well. It was then I determined to do some serious in-depth research on these golden granules from the beehive.

At that time, I was in a partnership involved with the stock market. We provided a highly successful and financially rewarding investment-advisory service. But once I started ferreting out and reading the scientific research and double-blind studies on the incredible potency of those little golden grains from the bees, I was well and truly hooked. I lost interest in the stock market, sold my share of the investment-advisory service, dissolved the partnership, and devoted myself full-time to the study of the products of the beehive.

It wasn't easy accumulating this material. Much of the research on the products of the beehive was (and still is) conducted in what were the Soviet bloc countries, although things have eased somewhat now. When I started my efforts in the mid-1970s, it took time, money, perseverance, and determination to persuade that closed scientific community to provide me with copies of its research reports. Once received, I still had to have them translated.

Yet, the more I found out, the more I wanted to know. I was aware I didn't have the whole story. According to published scientific reports, researchers in the laboratories of the world were making incredible discoveries about the characteristics of all the products of the bees. Everywhere but in the United States, there seemed to be agreement that bee products possess remarkable, near-miraculous, health-promoting properties.

In the 1970s, I became serious about searching out and chasing down everything there was to know about bee pollen, propolis, and royal jelly. In the beginning, I concentrated on bee pollen in particular. I put an assistant to work on the problem with an order that seemed to cover everything: *I want the best bee pollen in the world.* I had no idea that what I would discover would lead me to the founding of my own beehive-product company. Remember, this whole thing started out as a personal odyssey. But what I learned along the way was just too important to keep all to myself. I was sure you needed to know, too.

Knowing what I know now about the benefits of the bee's gifts—all can be called preventive medicine in the best sense of the term—I'm very thankful I persisted. Once you read this book and discover for yourself how easy it is to put the products of the beehive to work for you, I think you'll be glad, too.

1

THE HISTORICAL HONEYBEE

To haughty ladies of past centuries, amber ornaments and toiletry articles were as highly prized, and as costly, as those fashioned of gold. To David Grimaldi, assistant curator of the American Museum of Natural History in New York, a certain walnut-sized piece of translucent amber containing the fossilized remains of what he calls "the oldest bee known" is beyond price. This bit of amber has been dated at 80 million years, but the bee preserved inside it may be much older. Chemical analysis indicates the resin components producing this amber actually came from a family of early conifers that proliferated in the Cretaceous period, from 65 million to 135 million years ago. The grand sequoia of today is a relative of those early pines.

Propolis is often called bee glue. Bees, then as now, collect propolis, take it back to the hive, mix it with wax flakes they secrete, and use it to chink up holes. Because propolis is the strongest natural antibiotic and disinfectant known, the bees also use it to insure the interior of the hive remains hospital clean. If a foreign object too large for the housekeeping bees to remove contaminates the hive, it is coated heavily with propolis and sealed off. The bee embedded in the chunk of amber was undoubtedly on a propolis-gathering mission when she was caught and held fast in the sticky resinous sap of some ancient leaf bud.

The oldest preserved bee in the world is embedded in a piece of amber on display at the American Museum of Natural History, New York. It was discovered by David Grimaldi, assistant curator of the museum.

Prior to this stunning discovery, the oldest known preserved bee in existence was only about 45 million years old. However, authorities have long theorized that bees came into being at least 125 million years ago, when flowering plants began blossoming in profusion. Bees and plants are so dependent on one another for their very existence that experts say they must have "invented" one another. Many plants depend on the bees for the pollination, or fertilization, they require. Bees must have the carbohydrates from the nectar in the hearts of blossoms, as well as the proteins from the pollen. Fossilized remains of pollen, leaves, and even flowers have been dated back to when dinosaurs ruled the land, more than 125 million years ago.

Scientists determined some time back that bees have changed little in the past 80 million years. Now that finding has been revised. Entomologists who examined Grimaldi's fossilized bee discovered the wings and legs of this ancient creature are remarkably modern in design. The scientists point out that the structure of the hind legs shows this ancient bee carried pollen in exactly the same way bees do today. And they are still mystified that these little critters can fly. It has been scientifically established that it is aerodynamically impossible for those fragile gossamer wings, the same today as yesterday, to lift that heavy, ungainly body off the ground and carry it through the air in sustained flight. Fortunately for those of us who prize the products of the beehive, the bee herself doesn't know that.

The honeybee has been fulfilling her genetic programming since well before man first appeared on Earth. Somewhere back in the long-forgotten, misty recess of time, an early human somehow got a taste of honey. How did it happen? Perhaps a hive grew to such a great size that the branch of the tree to which it was fastened gave way. Perhaps the frightened colony swarmed elsewhere when its waxen metropolis cracked open as it crashed to the ground. But what inspired that first human to actually pick up a piece of broken comb, poke in a finger, take that first taste, and then greedily suck the comb clean?

However it may have happened, we do know that primitive humans not only fought the bees for their honey but also feasted royally on the bee pollen stored in the comb and even ate the eggs and larvae. Aboriginal tribes still feast on bee grubs and still regard bee pollen and honey as well worth the price of a few stings.

For millennia, man has been making use of the God-given products of the beehive. For example, writings over 2,000 years old reveal that Egyptian physicians called honey the universal healer. In ancient China, honey was used to treat victims of smallpox. The sticky stuff was smoothed over the entire body of the infected person. According to old records, the contagious and disfiguring disease was stopped in its tracks, and no pitting or scarring ensued. Ayurveda, India's ancient protocol for health and beauty, makes use of beehive products. And raw honey, rich and cloudy with bee-pollen particles and flecks of propolis, is said to have been a favored beauty potion of Cleopatra.

The bees even played a part in the glory days of the Roman Empire. Written records show conquering Roman legions carried pressed and dried cakes made of bee pollen, honey, and grain as travel rations. Modern chemical analyses show bee pollen alone contains nutrients sufficient to sustain life and maintain optimal health.

Royal jelly, still rare and difficult to secure, was prized by Oriental potentates as an aid to longevity and sexual prowess. Clinical research shows this hormone-charged royal "milk" of the bees really does stimulate cell and glandular activity.

Hippocrates (460–370 B.C.), long revered as the Father of Medicine, prescribed bee pollen and propolis as medicaments against many of the ills of his time. Hippocrates discovered the health-promoting properties of hive products by observing the favorable reactions of his patients. Today, we have scientific and medical studies that confirm the medicinal benefits of the bee's gifts, as well as many, many personal testimonials from those who know firsthand what hive products can do.

MYTHS AND MYSTERIES

There are many fanciful stories surrounding the origin of the honeybee. Some say the gods transformed the goddess Melissa into a bee and bestowed upon her the ability to reproduce without a mate. The ancient Greeks called bees the result of a mystical marriage between hornets and the Sun, a joining that was said to have been ordained and blessed by the gods on Mount Olympus.

Down through the ages, mankind has revered the bee. Greek legends tell how the infant god Zeus was hidden from the wrath of his father to protect his life. Safe in the cave where he was taken, Zeus was well nourished on goat's milk and raw honey provided by Melissa's bees. When four men entered the cave where the baby Zeus lay hidden, their leather armor mysteriously fell away and left them unprotected. Melissa's bees then ferociously attacked the naked men and drove them away, thus preserving the life of the great god Zeus. A Greek vase from around 540 B.C. immortalizes this mythical encounter. This vase is currently on display in a British museum. The legend says that after this selfless service to Zeus, bees were able to reproduce without the mating of male and female. This

A Greek vase circa 540 B.C. shows Melissa's bees driving off intruders threatening the infant Zeus.

tale is one of the earliest attempts to explain what the ancients regarded as the mystifying lifestyle of the bees.

TRUTH REVEALED . . . ALMOST

Because no one had ever seen a bee mating, it was long believed that bees were sexless and that baby bees somehow originated in flowers. Much later, it was acknowledged worker bees were born in the hive, but most people still believed drones at least came from flowers. This odd explanation didn't satisfy Aristotle, however. About 400 years before the birth of Christ, Aristotle discarded all the outmoded theories and came up with some explanations of his own. He was almost right.

Aristotle's observations finally revealed why a hive was populated exclusively by drones when the colony was lacking a ruler. When the ruler was in residence, the society was composed of both workers and drones. And it wasn't because drones were born in flowers either. Aristotle arrived at the obvious conclusion: Rulers bred other rulers and workers. When the ruler was absent, workers produced drones. Drones, which were not recognized as males, did not breed. And the large and well-formed ruler of the hive had to be the "Bee King." Because of the patriarchal and chauvinistic nature of the times, it was unthinkable to Aristotle that the ruler of anything should be a female. And there the matter rested for the next 200 years.

THE DEIFIED BEE

Still, mixed up in all the misrepresentations and legends, one fact stands out clearly. Almost without exception, every age has regarded the bee as a benefactor of mankind and accorded this little creature almost holy status.

The Bible, the Talmud, the Torah, the Koran, and the Code of Islam, along with the scrolls of the Orient, the writings of ancient Greece and Rome, the legends of the Russian and Slavic peoples, and even the relatively recent Book of Mormon (1830), all praise the industrious honeybee and her highly nutritious and healing beehive products.

The Little Bee:
Her Life and Times

Worker honeybees, females all, have different responsibilities during the various stages of their lives. This tale is fanciful but factual.

The tiny Apis mellifera *egg was just one of more than 2,000 eggs tucked in a brood cell that day by the queen mother. The little egg nested in its wax nursery as its nucleus absorbed the nutriments surrounding it. As a developing embryo, the little bee was soon exhibiting tiny buds of tissue that would become her antennae and mandibles. She would not need her antennae for some time yet, but her mandibles and maxillae, her feeding organs, were going to be very important very soon.*

When the little bee emerged as a larva, she was still a helpless baby without legs or wings. The nurse bees tended her, just as they cared for all the other newly hatched baby bees. Her body, less than a quarter of an inch long, was an eating factory. For three days, nurse bees fed her sips of diluted royal jelly, but this was the only time she would be allowed the royal milk. Her main nutriments were bits of richly nutritious pollen, often called bee bread, plus some raw honey.

When her metamorphosis was complete, the little bee split the fragile shell and stepped out as a half-inch-long adult. Like all worker bees, she had jaws that bit inward, special smell sensors in her antennae (with more than 2,000 sense plates), and jewel-bright eyes colorblind to red but able to detect ultraviolet rays invisible to humans. This ability enables bees to make their way in the darkness of the hive.

As an adult, the little bee took up her communal responsibilities within the hive immediately. There was no census taker, but her colony averaged around 30,000 worker bees like herself, between 500 to 2,000 males (drones), and a ruling queen bee.

The little bee's first chore consisted of cleaning up her own brood chamber. Then a day or so after her birth, she began helping the nurse bees feed developing larvae older than three days. With the other nannies, she fed the maturing grubs highly nutritious pollen stored in pantry cells near the brood comb.

A portrait of the little bee.

At six to twelve days of age, the little bee began secreting royal jelly, qualifying her to feed larvae younger than three days old. She had attained the status of fully fledged nursing bee. When the majestic queen bee came into the vicinity, all the nursing bees took turns serving the queen her regal diet of royal jelly and grooming her carefully.

When the little bee graduated from nursery chores, she joined the housekeeping staff. She dragged out a leaf that had blown in. Two aged bees had died, but they were too heavy for her to remove from the hive alone. The little bee and several sisters joined together in taking them out.

During this period in her life, the little bee took several orientation flights outside the hive, never going far. She joined the receiving bees and helped pack pollen in cells. She assisted in ripening nectar. Because she was now producing wax flakes, she also worked as a builder, repairing broken comb and patching up a few small cracks.

There is no day and night inside a hive. The colony buzzes with activity twenty-four hours a day. Once, an unusually frenzied humming and buzzing began vibrating through the hive. The colony had grown too large. Many of the sisters were preparing to follow the present queen as she flew forth to find a new home. The sisters remaining behind took no notice when the old queen left with a swarm of bees trailing behind her.

In domestic hives, the beekeeper annually slips out the aging queen and substitutes an already-impregnated young queen. Wild bees rear their own queens. A queen bee may live for five to six years or even longer. Bees instinctively raise queens when the hive becomes so crowded that swarming is necessary or when the aging queen no longer lays sufficient brood.

If you have ever doubted the old adage that you are what you eat, consider the queen bee. She is made queen, not born queen. The only difference between worker bees and their queen is diet. Both begin life as identical eggs, with identical genes, but only the eggs deposited in oversized, peanut-shaped queen cells are groomed to become queen mothers. The baby blue bloods are fed hormone-rich royal jelly and choice bits of the richest, most superior bee pollen. This special diet transforms these larvae into queens. Because there can only be one queen, the first royal to emerge quickly destroys all the other young queens still in their cells by stinging them repeatedly. Worker bees die after stinging, but a queen can use her stinger repeatedly.

The excitement in the little bee's hive was caused by two new queens emerging from their cells at the same time. As the two young queens squared off to fight to the death, all the members of the colony were frantic. Both new queens could be severely injured. A colony without a queen cannot survive. As the royal battle was joined, the worker bees hummed and buzzed nervously, tumbling over one another in their excitement and fear. When it became clear one queen *would prevail, the onlookers stung the weaker queen to death. The victorious new queen then quickly disposed of all the young queens still sleeping in their royal chambers.*

When she was around four days old, the virgin queen took her mating flight, the only time she would leave the hive. With her wings beating the air at 11,400 strokes per minute, she soared upward. Attracted by the heady scent of her pheromones, the males of the hive followed. One drone, the strongest and mightiest of all, reached her and impregnated her. Spermatozoa passed into her sperm reservoir. A single impregnation is sufficient to fertilize all the eggs a queen will lay in her lifetime. The queen was now ready to assume her role.

Within a few days of her mating flight, the new queen began laying brood. A queen mother will lay upwards of 2,000 eggs daily, the equivalent of more than half her own body weight. When her supply of sperm shows signs of exhaustion, the bees will raise a new crop of queens.

In our hive, the business of the colony resumed as before. When she turned twenty-one (days), the little bee went to work as a guard bee, flying patrol around the entrance of the colony. An unwary wasp found itself with more than it could handle. The wasp did not survive the assault for long, but many of the sisters gave their lives in this encounter. The barbs on the end of a bee's stinger insure the victim cannot pull out the bee's needle-sharp instrument of vengeance, but when the bee herself tries to withdraw her stinger, a portion of her abdomen goes with it and she dies. However, the stinger keeps pumping and delivers a full load of venom nonetheless.

Somehow a big, ugly beetle had made its way into the hive unnoticed, probably during the full alert when the wasp was destroyed. Within a millisecond, the intruder was surrounded by a dense cloud of angry, buzzing bees. His time in the hive was short, but this large beetle proved too heavy to drag out, even when many of the sisters clustered around to help. The dead beetle was quickly encased in a sarcophagus of Mother Nature's disinfectant, propolis. Once the alien was thickly covered with propolis, the antiseptic cleanliness of the hive was restored and preserved.

Because the temperature of the hive must be maintained at a near-constant 94°F, the little bee also helped air condition the colony. As the temperature climbed, more and more bees began fanning their stubby wings over droplets of water, sending cool breezes throughout the hive. During hot weather, the bees working inside the hive position themselves with space in between to allow dispersion of body heat. If it had been a cold, blustery winter day, the bees would have clustered together to release the metabolic heat necessary to keep the interior of their home snug and cozy.

One day when she was close to four weeks old, the little bee suddenly felt impelled to become a forager. A sister a little older than she came dancing excitedly into the hive with tremendous news. This sister had located a source of superior pollen and nectar, and was transmitting the location to the colony with a wag-tail dance, all the while emitting blips of sound of such low frequency as to be inaudible to human ears.

The little bee flew off to the new fields and settled on a blossom. As she sucked up the deliciously sweet nectar, her chubby little body became covered with golden pollen. On her way to the next flower, she quickly brushed the bright flecks of pollen into the pollen baskets on her rear legs and tamped them down. She instinctively visited only the most perfect and superior flowers, pollinating (fertilizing) as she went, thus insuring superior growth the following season. Very soon, her honey pouch was full and both her pollen baskets were loaded with tightly packed kernels of the rich, highly nutritive golden dust.

The little bee lived in a lopsided globe of a nest fastened high in the leafy branches of an old apple tree. Her hive was built in the ages-old way. It might have graced any other tree in any other field throughout history. The little bee found her way home by tracking the scent of her queen mother's pheromones. If she had been born into a beekeeper's colony, she would have entered the hive through a pollen trap, which would have gently relieved her of a portion of the contents of her pollen baskets. As it was, she accepted the assistance of the receiving sisters and flew right back out. Barely in her fourth week of life, the little bee had become a field forager. She made many more trips before darkness fell.

A beehive in an apple tree.

Foraging now dominated the little bee's life. For the next two weeks, she was a solitary harvester. In just one day, the little bee, together with her sisters, visited more than 250,000 blooms. To produce a single pound of honey, the foraging bees had to make around 37,000 trips to the fields.

The little bee was in the sixth week of her life when she crawled to the exit and discovered she couldn't make the flight. Her tattered, worn-out wings and aging body just wouldn't cooperate. Still trying, she worked her way laboriously to the edge and tumbled lifeless to the ground. She had fulfilled her programming. The little bee had accomplished the grand design set out for her and her sisters in the dawn of creation. She was gone, but her species—the remarkable honeybee—will continue until the world ends. As it was in the beginning, so it ever shall be.

We need to remember that, in times past, all honey was taken in the comb. It was therefore rich with bee pollen and bits of propolis. It bore no resemblance to the strained (sometimes diluted) honeys of today. For example, we are told DBSH, pronounced DE-vash, a favored Hebrew sweet of centuries ago, was a sticky, thick, syrupy combination of honey and bee pollen.

Hebrew scholars of the Torah, the Old Testament of the Christian Bible, say early translators mistakenly used "honey" in many scriptures in place of the more accurate phrase "products of the beehive." The experts of today explain that the Hebrew and Aramaic languages used by the original authors of certain of our holy books included names and phrases that were lengthy and cumbersome. Because those first translators of so long ago were most familiar with honey, they probably shortened the phrase "products of the beehive" to "honey" in accordance with their personal experience and in the interest of what they no doubt regarded as accuracy. Today's linguists also question the interpretation of "seed" in certain scriptures, insisting that a more accurate translation would be "pollen."

In light of these revelations, some familiar scriptures take on a whole new meaning. Genesis 1:29 is an example. It states, ". . . and God said, Behold, I have given you every herb bearing seed which is upon the face of all the earth, and every tree, in which is the fruit of a tree yielding pollen; to you it shall be for food." The Lord God gave man pollen for his food.

Genesis 43:11 is another example. This passage says, ". . . and their father Israel said unto them, if it must be so, now do this; take of the best fruits in the land in your vessels and carry down the man a present, a little balm, and a little honeycomb, spices and myrrh, nuts and almonds." The first exchange of gifts between nations recorded in the Bible involved the gifts Jacob (Israel) ordered carried to his son Joseph in Egypt when he sent his other sons forth to purchase food to alleviate the severe famine in Israel. These precious gifts included honeycomb and myrrh, the latter of which some modern authorities liken to propolis.

Another passage, Exodus 16:1–36, says, ". . . and the children of Israel did eat manna for 40 years until they came to a land inhabited; they did eat manna until they came into the borders of Canaan." It is written that "the taste of manna was like wafers made of honey." The experts of today say manna was pollen of the Tamarisk tree. God counseled the Israelites to eat manna fresh. Science teaches that the hot desert sun damages pollen, causing it to lose nutrients as it ages. Those ancient tribes of Israel survived forty years of wandering in the desert in perfect health because they ate the perfect food—manna, the pollen of the Tamarisk tree.

To continue our examples of Bible passages that take on new meaning, Luke 24:41–43 states, "Jesus said unto them, Have ye any food? and they gave Him a honeycomb and a piece of broiled fish; and He took it and did eat before them." The first foods the risen Jesus Christ ate after His resurrection were honey and bee pollen in the comb, and broiled fish.

And finally, Numbers 13:27 says, "We came unto the land whither Thou sentest us and surely it floweth with milk and honey and this is the fruit of it." According to modern Biblical linguists, the correct translation of this passage of scripture is, "We came unto the land whither Thou sentest us and surely it floweth with milk and all the products of the beehive and pollen is the fruit of it."

The Church of Jesus Christ of Latter Day Saints, more familiarly known as the Mormons, today still holds the honeybee in very high regard. In fact, if Brigham Young, second president of the church, had gotten his way, the state of Utah would instead be carrying the name Deseret, a term for honeybee from the sacred Book of Mormon signifying "industry." When Brigham Young led Mormon pioneers into Utah to escape the persecution church members suffered for their practice of polygamy, the settlement around the Great Salt Lake was named Deseret in honor of the hard-working honeybee. As governor of the territory, Young applied for statehood in 1849 under the name Deseret, but the application was denied. However, a beehive appears on the Great Seal of Utah, and many Mormon industries of today are honored with the name Deseret.

Traveling further back in time, we find that the Rig-Veda, the holy book of the Hindu religion, which was penned in Sanskrit between 2000 and 3000 B.C., talks of bees almost with awe. Vishnu, the powerful preserver and protector in the Hindu trinity of gods, is often symbolized as a blue bee on a lotus flower. Kama, the Hindu god of love, wields a bow with a string made of an entwined chain of bees. In cultures worshipping a goddess of fertility, variously called Venus, Diana, Ceres, Cybele, or Iris, bees were always considered sacred and were minor deities in their own right.

Spring fertility rites often used the bee as a symbol for the festivities. It's easy to understand why. Bees are seldom out and about during seasons of dormancy, when growth is scant and blossoms are nonexistent. But in spring, when the sun-warmed earth sends forth fragrant flowers full of nectar and pollen, the bees reappear and joyously go about their tasks. The mysterious dance of the scout bees that signals the location of rich sources of food and sustenance to the rest of the hive was mirrored in the frenzied dancing of those long-ago celebrants welcoming the arrival of spring.

The Roman god Bacchus, known to the Greeks as Dionysius, is one of the major deities credited with introducing the practice of keeping bees. Although this happy god—sacrificed to by the best-known party-goers of any century, the rowdy Romans—is most often associated with a touch of the grape, there's more reason to think the drink this legendary god would personally have favored was mead, or honey wine.

Another story purporting to explain how mankind came to keep bees credits Aristaeus, son of Apollo and Cyrene, with bringing the knowledge of beekeeping to mortals. Aristaeus was supposedly educated by the Muses, the nine Greek goddesses who were patrons of the arts. Perhaps it was this mythical relationship that led to bees being called the Birds of the Muses. It was long believed that should a bee touch a child's lips, that child would have magical abilities in the arts. Legend has it that bees kissed Sophocles, Plato, and the renowned Roman poet Virgil while they were yet in their cradles. The patron saint of beekeepers, Saint Ambrose, was said to have been so blessed by the bees as well.

In fact, though we seldom give it a thought, all mankind has been blessed by the bees.

MAN AND BEE—TOGETHER FOREVER

We have a mysterious kinship with the honeybee that cannot

be denied. What the bee does instinctively, we imitate poorly at best. Are not man and bee pleasured by the very same things? Do we not seek sweets for our table, as the bee seeks nectar in the hearts of flowers? Do we not take pleasure in sweet-smelling perfumes, as the bee is attracted to the heady scent of blossoms? Do we not select pleasing colors for our garments and surroundings, as the bee works in fields of colorful flowers? And, in this troubled modern world, who among us does not wish for the God-given ability to live in harmony with all others?

The world of the bee is rich with the myriad colors and sweet scents of flowers and blossoms. The bee keeps her house in an orderly manner and also maintains antiseptic cleanliness within. Each member of bee society lives in perfect harmony with every other. Bees harvest and store the food the colony needs to survive. In the animal kingdom, only the bee has such vital work to do. Without the bee's ability to carry the pollen that fertilizes plants and flowers, many species would fail to survive. The bee truly improves the environment and enriches her corner of the world with her presence.

It is impossible to accurately determine just how long humans have prized the hard-working little honeybee. In fact, if bees and flowers "invented" one another, what is the true relationship between man and bee? The ecologists of today reckon over 100,000 species of plants would become extinct without the pollinating work of the bee. Without these plants, life as we know it—perhaps all life—would become impossible. Early man could not have known that, of course. All the ancients cared about was securing a potful of honey and a bowlful of bee pollen, usually topped off with some bee grubs.

An ancient rock painting discovered near Valencia, Spain, deep inside what has come to be known as Cueva de la Arcana (Cave of the Spiders), shows a woman mounting a primitive ladder to gather honey from the waxen city a colony of honeybees has tucked into a hole in the side of a cliff. The experts say this cave painting dates back to the Mesolithic era (circa 10000–3000 B.C.). A watercolor copy painted by F. Venitez Mellado hangs in the Museo de Prehistoria in Valencia. Another rock painting still visible in the Arcana cave depicts early tribesmen

A rock painting dating back to the Mesolithic era, discovered in a cave near Valencia, Spain, shows an ancient woman gathering honey.

robbing wild bees. The homemade dyes fashioned by the unknown artists so long ago are faded with time, but the scenes are unmistakable.

In Egypt, with its highly advanced culture, the honeybee and the products of the hive were held in the highest esteem. As early as 3500 B.C., Egyptians chiseled a likeness of the honeybee on their monuments, painted scenes of beekeepers tending bees on the walls of their tombs, and recorded the life and times of this hard-working little creature in holy hieroglyphs inscribed on papyrus scrolls.

Down through the ages, honey, that delectable treat from the beehive, was sought after and relished. It was both medicine and

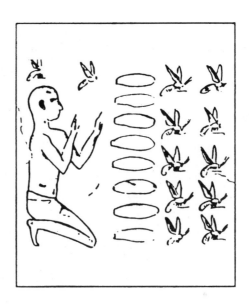

A painting in the tomb of Pa-Bu-Sa (circa 620 B.C.) in Thebes, Egypt, depicts an ancient beekeeper.

candy. If they could afford it, the Greeks of old gladly paid the three drachmas per quart strained honey cost back then. Not many could. The ancient Greek drachma was a coin containing about 4.3 grams of silver. In today's coin of the realm, that works out to around twenty-five dollars per quart of ancient honey.

Honey was the main sweet of the world for eons. It was in the fourth century B.C. that a general under the command of Alexander the Great wrote an accounting of a "wondrous reed which produces honey without the aid of bees." He had stumbled upon sugar cane, of course. The place was India. Sugar making had been practiced there as early as 3000 B.C. It was Christopher Columbus who brought sugar cane to the Americas. Today, many authorities name refined sugar a threat to health and are calling for a return to honey as a healthy, natural sweetener.

FACT OR FANCY?

People have always been fascinated by the buzzing society of the hive. Because they didn't know the facts, they invented fanciful stories to explain its mysteries. Northern Europeans believed bees were the souls of the dead, either returning to Earth or passing by on their way to the next world.

An early German legend insists bees were a gift to mankind by the Lord. This story says the life work of the bee is to provide wax for the immense number of candles needed to light the churches and cathedrals of the world for the glory of God.

An early Christian legend relates that the tears shed by Christ on the Cross turned into bees that flew away, bringing wholesome sweetness and food to humankind.

A French tale involving Jesus Christ explains it in still another way. When the Lord bathed in the River Jordan, the drops that fell from His body as He arose from the waters turned into bees. As the little bees were about to fly away, Christ bid them stay together and work for the benefit of mankind. Honeybees have been obeying this holy commandment ever since. Perhaps this lovely legend does contain a modicum of truth after all.

2

BEEKEEPING
PAST AND PRESENT

 Because they derive their nourishment from the nectar and pollen found in the hearts of blossoms, wild bees build their waxen cities wherever flowers flourish. They know no boundaries. Bees are found sipping nectar from high desert growth in springtime, in the arctic circle when the brief summer opens fragile blooms, and everywhere in between.

Down through the ages to the present, people have gone to extraordinary lengths to provide substitute homes for these little critters. Their aim, of course, has been to make it easier to harvest the fruits of the bees' hard work.

BEEKEEPING PAST

The beekeeper of old fashioned hives from a variety of materials. He then either sat back and hoped bees would take up residence or tried to capture a swarm. These manmade hives ranged from rudely hollowed-out logs, called bee gums, nailed to a tree to cylinders shaped from river clay to tightly woven straw "skeps," which resemble conical-shaped, upside-down straw baskets. Depending on the materials available, crude hives such as these are still in use. They can be found in jungle clearings in Africa, in the countrysides of many European and Asian nations, and even in the backwoods of America.

Beekeeping was revolutionized in the mid- to late-1800s when several important facts came to light. First, the Reverend L. L. Langstroth discovered the significance of "bee space" in the interior of the hive. He found bees require passageways of three-eights inch to one-half inch wide. If the space is smaller, the bees can't maneuver. If the space is larger, the bees promptly fill it up with comb. Langstroth designed the movable-comb hive, a rectangular "bee box" with vertical wooden frames on which the bees can build comb. When the top is lifted off, the frames the bees have obligingly filled with honeycomb can be easily removed for harvest and empty frames slipped in.

Second, Johannes Mehring, a German beekeeper, came up with the idea of giving the bees a head start. He supplied his hives with beeswax foundations on which his bees could build comb. Mehring imprinted a thin, flat sheet of beeswax with the precise outline of the octagonal cells of comb and fastened it to one of Langstroth's movable frames. Mehring's bees took to this idea immediately. All the bees had to do was add additional wax and draw the cells out to the proper depth. This is why we have straight, uniform honeycombs today instead of the hodgepodge conglomeration of odd-shaped combs bees build in the wild.

Third, a beekeeper by the name of Franz Hruschka, then living in Italy, found an easy way to remove the honey from the comb. Instead of cutting the comb apart and squeezing to separate the liquid honey from the wax, Hruschka put centrifugal force to work, and the honey extractor was born. Honey extracted this way is clear and free of hive debris. Best of all, after the honey is extracted, the same combs are returned to the hive. The bees promptly repair any broken cell walls and fill them up again with honey.

BEEKEEPING PRESENT

These three advances in the beekeeper's art heralded the modern age of beekeeping. Because they were so right, Langstroth's movable frames with carefully measured bee space, Mehring's foundation comb, and Hruschka's method of honey extraction are still in use, with one questionable advance. Today, beekeepers can choose from wax or *plastic* foundation combs. The bees don't seem to have a preference.

In a manmade bee box, the bees carry on their activities just as in the wild. They enter and leave at the bottom from a "landing pad." Their young are raised in the lower level, or "brood chamber." Honey and pollen (bee bread) are stored in the upper chamber. Additional sections, called supers, can be added to the top of the hive for still more honey and pollen storage. By lifting off the removable top, beekeepers can easily take out the honey-filled frames without disturbing the colony overmuch.

That was the extent of the helping hand man extended to the bee until the rediscovery of the other valuable products of the hive: bee pollen, propolis, and royal jelly. I stress *re*discovery because the renowned healers of antiquity employed all the

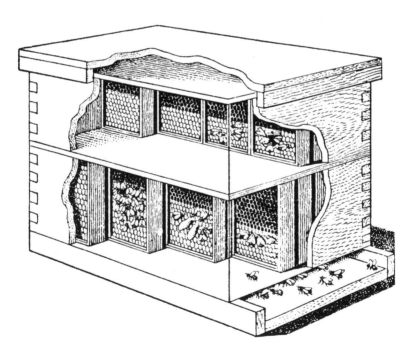

A cut-away drawing of a modern bee box.

products of the beehive. It was when the laboratories of the world community of nations confirmed bee pollen contains not only all the nutrients necessary in human nutrition but also medicinal qualities that an efficient way to harvest bee pollen for the use of humans became a necessity.

In the natural order of things, the pollen-foraging bee fills her honey sac on her way out of the hive. Once she selects a blossom, she settles herself and scrapes the loose, live pollen from the stamen with her jaws and front legs, moistening it with a dab of honey to keep it from blowing away. In her work, the bee becomes dusted with pollen. As she buzzes over to another flower, she uses her pollen combs to scrape the golden dust covering her stubby little body into her pollen baskets. The honeybee is admirably equipped for her task.

As the bee flits from flower to flower, the process is repeated over and over again. She nimbly scrapes the pollen from the heart of the flower, transfers it to her pollen baskets, and tamps it down. But many live pollen spores remain on her fuzzy coat. As she visits the next blossom, these spores brush off, and pollination is accomplished. Before her baskets are completely filled, a pollen forager will visit as many as 1,500 blossoms. A single granule of bee pollen contains from 500,000 to 5,000,000 live pollen spores.

When the pollen forager returns to the hive, she slips off the pollen kernel and, assisted by receiving bees, deposits it in the wax comb. Pollen, or bee bread, is a necessary part of the bee's diet. Pollen and honey are stored in separate groups of cells inside the honeycomb to be used as needed. Although these foods are not mixed together by the bee, raw honey in the comb is rich with pollen particles and bits of propolis. It bears little resemblance to most of the honey found in supermarkets.

Pollen is essential to the life and well-being of the hive. In order for beekeepers to harvest a portion of this live and potent substance, what they needed was a device that would dislodge a measure of the pollen as the bees enter the hive while permitting the bees to retain a sufficient portion of the life-giving golden dust for the maintenance of the colony. From 1959 to the present, many different pollen traps have come on the

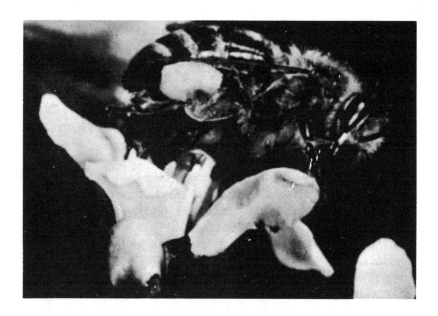

Time to head home. This weary bee has gathered pollen from as many as 1,500 flowers to fully fill her baskets.

market. The Universal Super Trap was developed by my company in 1984.

The Universal Super Trap consists of a box the same size as a standard bee box or hive. It is equipped with a series of scientifically engineered wire grids through which bees must pass to gain entrance to the colony. As a bee makes her way through the grids, approximately 60 percent of the pollen she's bringing home is gently brushed out of her pollen baskets. It falls through a screen into a pollen drawer situated beneath the trap.

The technology of the Universal Super Trap is all-important. It allows the bee to carry sufficient pollen through the grids and into the colony for the care and feeding of the hive population. It also insures the harvesting of the driest, cleanest pollen possible. Moisture-laden pollen from low-lying, humid locales ferments quickly or becomes moldy. This type of pollen must be heat-treated immediately to preserve it for use. But the necessary high-heat processing kills live enzymes and reduces

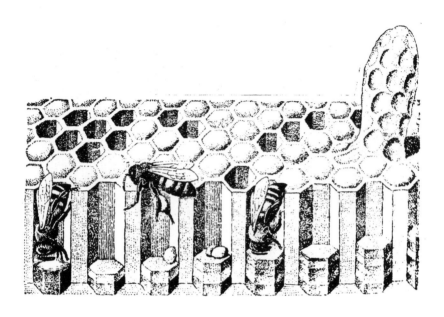

These worker bees are busily storing away freshly harvested bee-pollen balls and honey in the pantry cells of the hive. After the cells are completely filled, they are sealed off with a wax cap to preserve the food until it's needed. The peanut-shaped cell at the upper right represents the special extra-large cell in which a queen is reared.

the nutrient value considerably, transforming live pollen into a "dead" food.

When bee pollen is improperly stored and handled, it loses up to 76 percent of its nutritive value within twelve months. The best method for preserving fresh, live bee pollen is flash freezing at 0°F. Flash freezing preserves all the nutrients.

Permitting bee pollen to remain in the pollen drawer of the trap for as little as ten days results in nutrient loss or worse. Beekeepers who harvest for my company are required to gather bee pollen two times per week. They maintain a large chest-type freezer right alongside their honey extractor in their bee houses. My company requires all freshly gathered bee pollen to be immediately flash frozen in small batches.

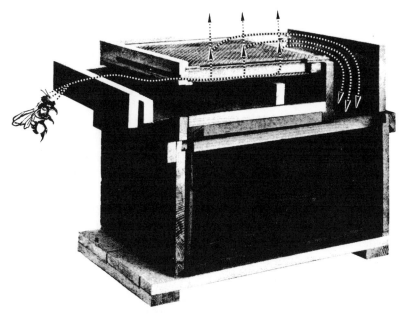

This cut-away view of the Universal Super Trap has arrows showing the passageways for the bees. The trap is in the middle position with the supers (top portion) of the hive removed. The pollen drawer is open. The side panel has been removed. The wax foundation comb, provided by the beekeeper, can be seen. Bees build onto the manmade foundation, drawing out comb for the storage of honey and pollen.

BEEKEEPING AS BIG BUSINESS

There are very few hive harvesters in the United States specializing in all the products of the bee. Most bee farms in the United States are maintained only for their honey production. Much of this honey ends up in supermarkets as a refined liquid sweet with all the bits of pollen and propolis strained out. Unfortunately, only a true, unrefined, raw honey can be classified as a nutritious food. Honey of this type is getting harder and harder to find. A few raw honeys still make their way into supermarkets, but the health-food store is the place where this unrefined liquid gold, cloudy and rich with suspended bee pollen, can definitely be found.

Because of her awesome powers of pollination, the honeybee is partner in many areas of agriculture. The experts say the

Beekeeping as an Absorbing Hobby

Compared to our ancestors, those of us who prize the products of the bee have it easy today. We don't even have to tend a garden. Honeybees forage wherever flowers grow. They have a flight range of twelve square miles. They are masters at seeking out sources of pollen and nectar.

If you're interested in beekeeping, it's easy to get started. Any library has books for the novice. Read them to learn the basics. Next, consider the population of your bee city. You can always revert to the old ways and capture a swarm. But, unless you really know what you're doing, this is risky business.

The best time to establish a hive is in the spring, when the sun has warmed the air and flowers are budding and blossoming. The best way to start is to purchase a bee colony and the necessary equipment from people in the business. A. I. Root of Medina, Ohio, and Dadant and Sons of Hamilton, Illinois, are highly reputable firms. Either can provide you with a complete bee colony.

Here's a "bee family portrait":

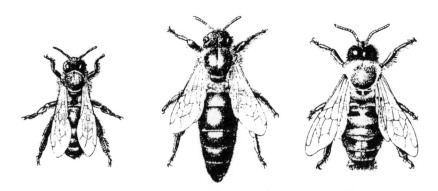

The three bees: worker (left), queen (center), and drone.

Worker bees are sexless, undeveloped females who do all the work of the colony. They gather the pollen, propolis, and nectar; ripen the honey; produce the royal jelly; feed and tend the queen; feed and rear the brood; secrete wax; repair and build the comb; ventilate the hive; and fight all the battles necessary to defend their home. The worker bees are the smallest in size, but they hold the power and regulate the ongoing work of the colony.

The queen is the unifying factor of the colony. Her pheromones fill the hive, and this scent identifies home to all her children. The worker bees will protect their queen mother with their lives. Even after an old queen is removed, her scent lingers.

Because the queen's lifetime diet is hormone-rich royal jelly, she is the only perfect, fully evolved female in the hive. She is larger than the worker bees, but her wings are proportionately shorter. Her only job is to lay eggs and perpetuate the species. A colony without a queen will not survive. As soon as workers tidy up nursery cells and line them with Nature's disinfectant, propolis, the queen fills them with brood again. She lays up to 2,000 eggs per day. To facilitate the deposit of eggs in brood cells, the queen's abdomen tapers to a point.

Drones, the male members of the colony, have a shorter and thicker body than the queen. Their wings reach the entire length of their abdomens. Drones do not do any work, but don't blame the poor guys: they have no stingers and no equipment for gathering pollen, propolis, or nectar. They are totally dependent on their sisters, the workers. The drones' only purpose is to mate with a newly born queen on her mating flight. However, because beekeepers requeen their hives every year by purchasing a young, fully impregnated queen, drones in domestic hives are out of a job. The number of drones in a wild hive varies according to the time of year. To make sure the colony survives the cold, dark days of winter, the workers drive the drones from the hive at this time of year. Stored food is too precious to share during cold months.

When you purchase a bee colony, your queen will arrive in a little wooden box. The entrance to the royal traveling case will be plugged with a sugary bee candy. By the time the workers nibble through the candy, the queen's pheromones will permeate the hive and the queen will be accepted by her stepchildren. Within eight weeks, all the stepchildren will have joined the dearly departed.

Old-time beekeepers grow lyrical about the pleasures of beekeeping. They tell of delights most will never experience; of enjoying a piece of fresh comb dripping with honey; of scooping up a handful of bee pollen to munch as they tend their hives; of nipping off a piece of warm, waxy propolis to chew on. Their eyes grow soft as they talk of the soothing buzz of a busy colony on a hot summer day. Some call this hum the finest accompaniment to a drowse in the shade the good Lord ever devised.

difference in yields in fields pollinated by bees can amount to hundreds of millions of dollars per year.

Some giant bee yards maintain thousands of colonies for the single purpose of fertilizing various crops. In the trade, they are known as migrating beekeepers. Farmers contract with such firms for the services of their bees. Bee boxes are carefully loaded as high as twelve deep on trucks, tied down securely, and transported to various sites around the country. These traveling beehives are then placed near fields of food crops. Once a particular crop has been pollinated, the migrating bee-keeper can load up his hives and truck them to other fields in season.

Because it would be a disaster of huge proportions if the populations of these hives were exposed to dangerous agribiz chemicals, migrating beekeepers have to know the practices of the farmer or farming conglomerate they are servicing. Migrating beekeepers are extremely careful to place their hives only with those who use chemicals that pose no danger to their valuable bees.

3

BEE POLLEN

 In spite of the many books and articles on bee pollen that have been published during the last ten years, there are still some people who aren't sure exactly what bee pollen is. The woman in charge of consumer inquiries at my company calls her department the Weird Letter Office. She tells me one person wrote the company a serious, otherwise very literate letter that asked, "Does bee pollen come from outer space?" Another writer asked, "Is bee pollen the poop of the bee?"

And, hard as it may be to believe, a newspaper article published as recently as January 15, 1988, states, in part, "Bee pollen seems to have a little bit of everything that's good for you. And it's yummy. Just don't be put off by the fact that bee pollen comes from bee excrement."

Talk about *mis*information.

WHAT IS POLLEN?

Pollen is the male seed of flowers. It is required for the fertilization of the plant. The tiny particles consist of 50/1,000-millimeter corpuscles, formed at the free end of the stamen in the heart of the blossom. Every variety of flower in the universe puts forth a dusting of pollen. Many orchard fruits and agricultural food crops do, too.

There are two types of pollen. Anemophile pollens are the wind-carried type. As breezes blow, they are sent helter-skelter through the air. These wind-carried pollens, which a few varieties of plants depend on for fertilization, are the ones that cause such distress to allergic individuals who suffer from, for example, hay fever or rose fever. The allergens that these pollens carry tickle the nose, trigger sneezing attacks, cause the eyes to swell and itch, and generally make life miserable for those who are allergic.

Entomophile pollens are the other type of pollen. They hitch a ride on insects, primarily honeybees, who forage among their blossoms. These pollens are heavier and of a different variety than the wind-carried pollens. Plants that produce entomophile pollens must have the help of the bees in order to be sure of fertilization. Entomophile pollens never become airborne and are not the culprits in allergic reactions.

As a matter of fact, bee pollen is a very effective treatment for seasonal pollen-induced allergies—indeed, all allergies. There is very good news for allergy sufferers everywhere. Please see page 61 for a discussion of the advances in this field.

WHAT IS BEE POLLEN?

Bee pollen is simply entomophile pollen with a very important touch of "magic" added by the bee. Gathering pollen is not as easy as it sounds. Once a honeybee arrives at a flower, she settles herself in and nimbly scrapes off the powdery loose pollen from the stamen with her jaws and front legs, moistening it with a dab of the honey she brought with her from the hive. The enlarged and broadened tarsal segments of her legs have a thick trimming of bristles, called pollen combs. The bee uses these combs to brush the gold powder from her coat and legs in midflight. With a skillful pressing movement of her auricle, which is used as a rammer, she pushes the gathered gold into her baskets. Her pollen baskets, surrounded by a fringe of long hairs, are simply concave areas located on the outside of her tibias. When the bee's baskets are fully loaded,

This bee's baskets are loaded with floral gold.

the microscopic golden dust has been tamped down into a single golden grain, or granule.

One of the most interesting facts about bee pollen is that it cannot be synthesized in a laboratory. Mother Nature is keeping secrets from us. When researchers take away a bee's pollen-filled comb and feed her manmade pollen, the bee dies, even though all the known nutrients are present in the lab-produced synthesized food. Many thousands of chemical analyses of bee pollen have been made with the very latest diagnostic equipment, but there are still some elements present in bee pollen that science cannot identify. The bees add some mysterious "extra" of their own. These unidentifiable elements may very well be the reason bee pollen works so spectacularly against so many diverse conditions of ill health.

Honeybees do double duty. They are programmed to gather pollen and carry it back to the hive as food for the colony. However, even more important as far as humans are concerned, they are also responsible for the pollination of more than 80 percent of green growing things. In the grand scheme of life, we can conjecture that the bees' primary duty is almost certainly to accomplish pollination.

As bees buzz from blossom to blossom, microscopic pollen particles coat their stubby little bodies so densely that they sometimes look like little yellow fuzz balls. When they arrive at the next flower, a portion of the live golden dust is transferred to that blossom and pollination is accomplished.

When the Creator wrote out the job description for the bees, their number-one responsibility was the pollination of plants. This they neatly accomplish in the course of collecting food for the colony. Without the pollen-carrying honeybee, many species of plants would fail to be fertilized and would die out. It isn't only flowering plants that depend on the services of the bee either. I think you'll agree the world would be less pleasant without beautiful, sweet smelling flowers, although we humans could survive without them. But, without the food crops bees pollinate, mankind might well be in danger of extinction.

This pollen-foraging bee is in midflight. Her pollen baskets are fully packed. A portion of the tiny pollen particles covering her body will dust off on the next blossom and pollination, or fertilization, will be completed.

RESEARCH FROM AROUND THE WORLD

In spite of all the solid documentation of the many benefits of bee pollen and the other products of the beehive, American scientists have shown little interest in them. The following material comes primarily from the work of scientists and medical researchers in other parts of the world. In most instances, the work was published only in the language of origin, although a few papers do carry an English-language abstract of a few sentences. For the most part, a full translation was necessary in order to fully comprehend the subject matter.

Because I thought it important, I took on the task of seeking out the researchers working with beehive products, negotiated to secure copies of important published papers, and commissioned the necessary translations. This ongoing effort has been both time-consuming and costly. But one of my main goals has always been to produce the best beehive products in the universe.

The papers I report on in the following pages are heavy with scientific and medical terminology. Most are written in highly technical terms. I realize that scientific studies make dull, dry reading, no matter how important the subject matter may be. To make this material easier to deal with, I have separated the wheat from the chaff, condensed and rephrased pertinent excerpts, and sprinkled in a few direct quotes for solid documentation.

Settle back and relax. This is where you discover the scientific basis for all my beliefs about the beehive products and the reason my company has been receiving so many letters of testament over the years. Space considerations make it impossible to give you a review of all the research I have on file. But, brief as it is, this synopsis is enlightening and eye-opening. I think you're going to be surprised at the number of diverse conditions bee pollen seems to successfully conquer.

COMPLETE NUTRITION

From the Royal Society of Naturalists of Belgium and France comes the almost poetically entitled work "The Secrets of the Life of Bees." Chemical analyses from research labs all over the world show that bee pollen provides all the nutrients humans need for life support. Because the article from the Royal Society is so detailed, I selected it to report on the nutritive value of bee pollen.

Originally written in French, this twelve-page article by Robert Delperee ably demonstrates the ability of bee pollen to completely sustain life and favorably influence the body. The chemical composition table on page 41 is an important part of this landmark report.

In clinical tests around the world, bee pollen has been established as a "complete food." A complete food is defined as a foodstuff that provides all the nutrients necessary for life and health. The nutritional tests conducted by the Royal Society of Naturalists confirm this basic premise. According to Delperee, "The nutritional tests supervised by the station at Bures on hundreds of mice have demonstrated that pollen is a complete food, that it is possible to let several generations be born and live without the least sign of distress while nourishing them exclusively on pollen."

Because the life cycle of mice is short, these little animals are favored by scientists investigating the long-term effects of a substance. The lucky mice fed bee pollen in this particular study were uniformly energetic and lively. They remained healthy throughout their lives, gave birth to healthy offspring, and demonstrated good resistance to disease. Before the study was ended, four complete generations of mice were born and lived a normal life span on a diet of bee pollen.

Also according to Delperee, "Bee pollen contains all the essential components of life. The percentage of revivifying and rejuvenating elements in bee pollen is remarkable for exceeding those present in brewer's yeast and wheat germ. Bee pollen corrects the failings due to deficient or unbalanced nutrition, common in the customs of our present-day civilization of consuming incomplete foods, often with added chemical ingredients, which expose us to physiological problems as various as they are numerous."

Nutrient deficiencies—and all the health problems they cause—are recognized worldwide as a growing problem. Delperee was not talking about malnutrition or starvation caused by famine, which is a real threat to many. He was pointing to the proliferation of nutrient-poor, additive-laden manufactured foods.

Chemical Composition of Bee Pollen
Quantitative Analysis of Valuable Components

Analysis of Amino Acids as percentage of total dry weight	
Arginine	4.4–5.7
Histadine	2.0–3.5
Isoleucine	4.5–5.8
Leucine	6.7–7.5
Lysine	5.9–7.0
Methionine	1.7–2.4
Phenylalanine	3.7–4.4
Threonine	2.3–4.0
Tryptophan	1.2–1.6
Valine	5.5–6.0

Analysis of Vitamins and Hormones in micrograms/gram	
Thiamine	5.75–10.8
Riboflavin	16.3–19.2
Nicotinic acid	98–210
Pyridoxine	0–9
Pantothenic acid	3–51
Biotin	0.1–0.25
Folic acid	3.4–6.8
Lactoflavine	0.2–1.7
Vitamin A: Alpha/beta carotene	1.53
Vitamin B_2	16.3–19.2
Vitamin C	152–640
Vitamin D	0.2–0.6
Vitamin E	0.1–0.32
Inositol	30–40
Vitamin B_{12}	.0002

Analysis of Mineral Substances and Trace Elements as percentage of ash	
Potassium	20–45
Magnesium	1–12
Calcium	1–15
Copper	0.05–0.08
Iron	0.01–0.3
Silicon	2–10
Phosphorus	1–20
Sulfur	1
Chlorine	0.8
Manganese	1.4

Some Substances Isolated From Pigments

Flavoxanthine; xanthophyll epoxide; carotene; epiphasic carotenoids; flavonols; ethylic ether; quercitin; zeaxanthine; lycopene crocetin.

Analysis of Other Components
as percentage of total dry weight

	Range	Average
Water	3–4	
Reducing sugars	7.5–40	20
Non-reducing sugars	0.1–19	5
Starches and other carbohydrates	0–22	
Etheric extract (volatile fatty acids falsify the quantitative analysis of humidity beyond 70°C)	0.9–14	4.5
Proteins	7–35	20
Free amino acids (almost constant levels)		10
HGH (Human Growth Hormone) Factor	Not measured	
Hormones (gonadotropic and estrogenic)	Not measured	
Rutin	Not measured	
Ash	1–7	3

In affluent societies, whole foods are often bypassed in favor of processed and packaged foods, which are often lacking important nutrients. If you haven't been feeling up to par lately, you might want to take a careful look at your diet.

The bottom line is that bee pollen is one of Nature's best whole foods. I'm not recommending that you immediately pitch all the food in your kitchen cupboards. But, isn't it interesting to know you could live in the most desolate place in the universe and—just as long as you had a beehive or two—dine exclusively on bee pollen for uncounted generations?

Is bee pollen the answer to the periodic famines that plague some of the underdeveloped countries of the world? Because it is a complete food, Dr. Günther Vorwohl thinks it could be. Vorwohl's lecture on this subject, entitled "Pollen and Honey," was well received at the Apiarist Convention, held in Sontra, Germany, in October 1976. In translation from the original German, the speech affords us an inside look at this workable and innovative approach to the problem of world hunger. According to Vorwohl:

> Because it contains all the nutrients needed to sustain life, bee pollen is being used on an ever larger scale for human nourishment and health. In this connection, two considerations are of vital importance.
>
> As we all know, the human population on Earth is continuously increasing. Standard food production cannot keep up with the population explosion. Much of humanity is threatened by hunger. Added to inadequate general food production, there is the more pronounced insufficiency of foods rich in proteins. Large portions of the world are malnourished in this respect, in that their food does not contain sufficient protein.
>
> Science teaches that bee pollen contains many substances that combine to make it a healthy, nutritious, complete food. There are numerous reports from medical experience that conclusively show the benefits of bee pollen exceed that of a simple food item. Bee pollen contains all the essential amino acids we must eat every day, be-

cause the human body cannot manufacture them. Mixed bee pollens compare favorably to other valuable protein foods, including eggs, cheese, and soybeans. And the bees do most of the work.

It is time to focus world attention on the dietary use of bee pollen, the protein food of the bees. We must harvest more and more of this food from the hive and teach others to do the same, especially in the malnourished and famine-stricken areas of the world. Bee pollen can be the answer to world hunger.

There is so much material on the complete nutrition of bee pollen that I bring you only the concluding paragraph of an article, "On the Physiological and Therapeutic Effects of Various Pollen Extracts," published in April 1957 by *La Revue de Pathologie Generale et de Physiologie Clinique (Review of General Pathology and Clinical Physiology)*. R. Chauvin sums up his research as follows:

Conclusion: Bee-gathered pollens are rich in proteins, free amino acids, vitamins, including B-complex, and folic acid. In addition, they contain variable quantities of an antibiotic shown potent against *E. coli* and *Proteus*, as well as a substance that significantly accelerates healthy growth of mice receiving a complete and balanced diet from other sources. The acceleration of growth is tied to a modification of the metabolism of carbohydrates.

In human nutrition, the effect of bee pollen acts favorably in the intestines, on the hemoglobin level of the blood, and in the renewal of strength in convalescents and the aged.

All around the world, scientists and medical researchers praise the nutritive properties of bee pollen. Without going into the same depth of detail I did above, I would like to present still more documentation.

According to researchers at the Institute of Apiculture, Taranov, Russia, "Honeybee pollen is the richest source of vitamins found in Nature in a single food. Even if bee pollen had none of its other vital ingredients, its content of rutin alone would justify taking at least a teaspoon daily, if for no other reason than strengthening the capillaries. Pollen is extremely rich in rutin and may have the highest content of any source, plus it provides a high content of the nucleics RNA [ribonucleic acid] and DNA [deoxyribonucleic acid]."

Alain Callais, Ph.D., Academy of Agriculture, Paris, France, says, "Bee pollen is a complete food and contains many elements that products of animal origin do not possess. Bee pollen is more rich in proteins than any animal source. It contains more amino acids than beef, eggs, or cheese of equal weight. Bee pollen is particularly concentrated in all elements necessary for life."

And according to Dr. G. J. Binding of the British Empire, "Bee pollen is the finest, most perfect food. It is a giant germ-killer in which bacteria simply cannot exist. The health restoring properties of honeybee pollen have been proven time and time again. Honeybee pollen not only builds up strength and energy in the body, but gives increased resistance to infection."

MEDICAL MIRACLES

This next paper, "The Products of the Hive" by R. Borneck, deals with several specific benefits of bee pollen as exhibited in ongoing research. Published in 1977 in *Techniques du Directorat des services Veterinaires*, out of Paris, it includes the following:

> Products of the Hive—Pollen: In the last decade, we have seen beehive products return to the place of honor they held in past ages. Today, biologists, biochemists, doctors, researchers, and scientists are studying their uses in medicine and human nutrition.
>
> Researchers have demonstrated that there is a substance in bee pollen that inhibits the development of numerous harmful bacteria. Experiments have shown bee pollen contains an antibiotic factor effective against salmonella and some strains of colibacillus. On the clinical

level, studies have shown that a regulatory effect on intestinal function can be attributed to bee pollen. The presence of a high proportion of cellulose and fiber in pollen, as well as the existence of antibiotic factors, all contribute to an explanation for this efficacious effect.

Working with lab animals has demonstrated that the ingestion of bee pollen has a good effect on the composition of blood. A considerable and simultaneous increase of both white and red blood cells is observed. When bee pollen is given to anemic patients, their levels of hemoglobin [oxygen-carrying red blood cells] increase considerably. In humans, it has also been observed that the ingestion of bee pollen brings a beneficial overall effect to convalescents and the aged. When bee pollen is added to the diet, strength returns rapidly and a characteristic euphoria is noted.

From Romania comes a paper by G. Calcaianu and F. Cozma entitled "Treatment With Bee Products of the Behaviour Troubles in Young People in the Period of Puberty and Teen-Age." Authored in the mid-1970s, it offers special insight into the care and feeding of troubled youngsters, a subject sometimes overlooked in the United States.

It's a medical fact that the human body undergoes many biological and hormonal changes throughout the teen years. Because their bodies are changing so rapidly, young people often manifest antisocial behavior during this period. Factor in a fondness for junk food and poor dietary habits—many teens don't take in the nutrients needed to support their bodies adequately during the hormonal shifts of puberty. Add in peer pressure to conform to the norm, especially bad if what's considered normal is taking drugs, drinking alcohol, and smoking tobacco and/or marijuana. In addition, some teens don't have supportive, loving parents and are totally on their own, while others are under extreme parental pressure to do well, indeed, to excel, in school. With all those biological changes to cope with on top of everything else, it's easy to understand why so many teenagers today are under stress.

The Romanian study involved sixty-seven youngsters between fifteen and eighteen years old. The teens were selected because they were troubled. Many were angry and disruptive. They were actively rebelling against family, teachers, and authority figures. Some refused to show any interest or feeling whatsoever, even when punished. They were withdrawn, closed within themselves. In short, each of these young people was disturbed and had been labeled a behavior problem.

The object of this study was to determine if dietary changes would result in behavioral changes. These youngsters were given dietary supplements of bee pollen, royal jelly, and honey. Insofar as was possible, their diets were monitored.

Complete nutrition did make a difference. The shifts in attitude were gradual, but the gains were steady. As these youngsters' bodies (and brains) were provided with necessary nutrients, their minds became clearer. Their antisocial behavior slowly changed to socially acceptable behavior. As the teens began to feel better, they became calmer and less stressed.

Drs. Calcaianu and Cozma were satisfied that the results of this study proved the validity of their original premise. They concluded their paper by saying, "The results of our investigation showed us that, with adequate dietary therapy, we can prevent some behavioral troubles. In periods of biological crisis, such as during puberty and the teen years, the young body needs foods with a rich content of active, whole nutrients. Given regularly, bee products—pollen, royal jelly, and honey—lead to favorable results."

An article entitled "A Summary of Clinical Tests Concluded With Bee Pollen and Other Substances," from a 1977 issue of the German publication *Naturheilpraxis*, confirms these results. According to the article, "Bee-pollen preparations increase mental work performance and stimulate blood circulation in the brain. In five out of eight children who were mentally lazy and doing poorly in school, mental performance and grade point average improved significantly after they took bee pollen for twelve weeks.

"In ten adult patients, faulty memory and lack of concentration were improved after their diets were supplemented with bee pollen for three months," the article continues. "It is important to note that, in elderly patients especially, a change for the better is always observed."

In this same article, it is reported that bee pollen in the diet acts to normalize cholesterol and triglyceride levels in the blood: "Upon the regular ingestion of bee pollen, a reduction of cholesterol and triglycerides was observed. High-density lipoproteins (HDL) increased, while low-density lipoproteins (LDL) decreased. A normalization of blood serum cholesterol levels was observed in forty patients."

One of the most important articles ever published on bee pollen comes from our own United States Department of Agriculture. This article, entitled "Delay in the Appearance of Palpable Mammary Tumors in C3H Mice Following the Ingestion of Pollenized Food," is the work of William Robinson of the Bureau of Entomology, Agriculture Research Administration. It was published in the *Journal of the National Cancer Institute* way back in October 1948, over four decades ago. According to the article, Dr. Robinson started with mice that had been specially bred to develop and subsequently die from tumors. He explains, "The age at which mice of this strain developed tumors ranged from 18 to 57 weeks, with an average appearance at 33 weeks. Tumor incidence was 100 percent."

The pollen used in this study was supplied by the Division of Bee Culture and, according to the report, "was the bee-gathered type." One group of mice was fed mice chow only; another group was fed mice chow with the addition of bee pollen at a ratio of 1 part bee pollen to 10,000 parts food.

Dr. Robinson's article states, "Particular attention was given to the weight of the treated animals, since underweight can in itself bring about a delay in tumor development. No decrease in weight occurred in the animals receiving the pollenized food. Instead, a slight but fairly uniform increase was noted, possibly due to a nutritional factor in pollen."

In his summary, Dr. Robinson reveals the dramatic results: "In the untreated mice [the mice not given bee pollen], mammary tumors appeared as expected at an average of 31.3 weeks. Tumor incidence was 100 percent. In the postponement series [the mice given bee pollen], the average [onset of tumors] was 41.1 weeks, a delay of 9.8 weeks being obtained. Seven mice in this series were still tumor-free at 56 to 62 weeks of age, when the tests were terminated."

I would like to emphasize that these mice were especially bred to die from cancerous tumors. Without the protection of bee pollen in their food, the mice developed tumors and died right on schedule.

Dr. Robinson concludes his article by saying, "It is suggested that the use of the extracted and standardized active principle from bee pollen might produce greater postponement. These experiments were based on the postulation that bee pollen contains an anticarcinogenic principle that can be added to food."

Given the fact that cancer is the number-two killer in the United States (heart disease is number one), we can all certainly agree that this is an electrifying article. What happened from it? Nothing. Even the National Cancer Institute, which published it, failed to follow up on this very promising line of research. It was dropped with no explanation.

But other medical detectives remain enthusiastic about the properties bee pollen displays against this dread killer. For example, according to L. J. Hayes, M.D., in a 1958 issue of *L'Apiculteur haut-chinois*, "Bees sterilize pollen by means of a glandular secretion that is antagonistic to tumors." This particular effect has also been noted by the renowned Russian science writer Naum Ioyrish, author of *Bees and People*.

Sigmund Schmidt, M.D., of the Natural Health Clinic, Bad Bothenfelds, Germany, says, "Bee pollen contains all the essential elements for healthy tissue and may well prove to be the natural cancer preventive all the world is seeking."

And Ernesto Contreras, M.D., noted cancer specialist and medical director of the Ernesto Contreras Hospital, Tijuana, Mexico, states, "In the biological treatment of cancer, proper nutrition is gaining more and more importance. To my knowledge, there is no better and more complete natural nutrient than honeybee pollen. Properly used, it should always give the expected results. A shift to natural nonaggressive agents in the management of cancer is mandatory for better results and happier patients."

More good news comes from the University of Vienna, where Dr. Peter Hernuss and colleagues conducted a study of twenty-five women suffering from inoperable uterine cancer. Because surgery was impossible, the women were treated with chemotherapy. The lucky women given bee pollen with their food quickly exhibited a higher concentration of cancer-fighting immune-system cells, increased antibody production, and a markedly improved level of infection-fighting and oxygen-carrying red blood cells (hemoglobin). These women suffered less from the awful side effects of chemotherapy as well. Bee pollen lessened the terrible nausea that commonly accompanies the treatment and helped keep hair loss to a minimum. The women also slept better at night. The control group receiving a placebo did not experience comparable relief.

A 1978 Yugoslavian paper entitled "Therapeutic Effects of Melbrosin in Irradiation Diseases" by I. Osmanagic, D. Biljenski, and N. Mavric supports the results achieved at the University of Vienna. (Melbrosin is a European preparation of bee pollen, royal jelly, and honey.) In this study, eighty-four female patients undergoing radiation for gynecological cancer were divided into two groups. The ages ranged from thirty-four to seventy-one. All the women suffered secondary symptoms as a result of the radiation treatment. In Europe, this condition is called x-ray disease. The symptoms included a lack of energy, nausea, vomiting, diarrhea, anorexia (loss of appetite), headache, insomnia, tachycardia (irregular heartbeat), elevated temperature, and severe fatigue. In some patients, the symptoms of x-ray disease became so severe that the radiation was temporarily stopped to give the women time to regain a measure of strength.

Osmanagic, Biljenski, and Mavric acknowledge that almost every patient undergoing radiation treatment will develop x-ray disease. They note that radiation causes decomposition of tissue, both cancerous and healthy, resulting in a proliferation of toxins within the body. The doctors state, "As there is no specific medicine for x-ray disease, we have decided to use natural bioactive bee-product substances."

The results were dramatic. According to the paper's conclusion, "After taking the preparation, 30.5 percent of the patients had no sign of fatigue; 66.7 percent felt light fatigue; only 2.8 percent still complained of severe fatigue; 38.9 percent no longer suffered from anorexia; 41.6 percent exhibited light anorexia; 8.3 percent, moderate anorexia; 44.4 percent suffered no longer of nausea; in 50 percent, nausea was reduced to the mildest form; in only 5.6 percent did the intensity of nausea remain unchanged.

"The bee products manifested a significantly positive effect in the morbid state caused by irradiation. After we calculated the irradiation index, it was possible to conclude that improvement was obtained in 88.8 percent of the cases. This is indisputable proof of the positive effects achieved by bee products."

From the Agronomic Institute, Faculty of Zootechnics, Romania, comes a report showing the immune-strengthening effects of bee pollen. Given the state of the world today, this paper should be of great interest to medical science as well as the rest of us. According to the report, "Comparative Studies Concerning Biochemical Characteristics of Beebread as Related to the Pollen Preserved in Honey" by Drs. E. Palos, Z. Voiculescu, and C. Andrei, "An increase has been recorded in the level of blood lymphocytes, gamma globulins, and proteins in those subjects given pollen in comparison with control groups. The most significant difference occurred in lymphocytes. These results thus signify a strengthening in the resistance of the organic system."

Just in case you don't have a medical dictionary handy, I'll explain why this is an important finding. Lymphocytes are the white blood cells that are the "soldiers" of the immune system. They are responsible for ridding the body of injurious and harmful substances, including infected or diseased cells, mutant and cancerous cells, viruses, metabolic trash, and so on. Gamma globulin is a protein formed in the blood, and our ability to resist infection is closely related to this protein's activity.

A paper read at the International Symposium on Apitherapy entitled "Pollen Preparations and Their Impact on Immunological Reactions of Test Mice" confirms the results reported above. We have only a brief English-language abstract of this 1974 paper, but it says, "The fact that the immunological reaction is stronger [in mice given bee pollen] compared with the reaction of animals given only commercially prepared food may be attributed to pollen's nutritive effects. An addition of bee pollen to enriched food stimulated the immunological reaction, which may be due to the presence of specific stimulating factors in the bee pollen grains."

To my mind, any substance that can measurably boost the defensive systems of the body should be included in the diet. What do you think?

REPRODUCTIVE AND SEXUAL FUNCTION

There are many written reports on the powerfully potent action honeybee pollen exerts on a variety of sexual dysfunctions. This perfect food from the beehive seems to have the miraculous ability to restore and rejuvenate tired or aging sex glands, both male and female. According to the reports, this is because bee pollen contains natural hormonal substances that stimulate and nourish the reproductive systems. Sexual stamina and endurance also seem to be increased.

The natural hormonal substances in bee pollen that work these wonders have been isolated and identified. In clinical work, researchers have been able to document the glandular boost and therapeutic effects bee pollen provides. For example, Dr. Izet Osmanagic of the University of Sarajevo has documented the effects of bee pollen on reduced sexual potency. According to his paper "Effects of Melbrosin in Cases of Reduced Sexual Potency," which has been translated from the Slavic:

> Sexual impotence in men is far more frequent than is generally thought, as many men who suffer from it are reluctant to consult a doctor. We established contact with the patients studied in this report through the person most concerned about a man's impotence, his wife. These

women consulted the Gynecological Clinic at the University of Sarajevo about infertility. It was soon discovered that, in many cases, the man was to blame. We studied 40 men between 20 and 52 years of age. In most cases, the patients had lived in sterile marriages for two or more years.

Seventy-five percent of the men were found to be suffering from sperm deficiencies. Our patients took between 80 and 160 capsules of the bee-pollen preparation, the daily dose being two capsules. During the two- to three-month periods of taking the preparation, patients were interviewed and sperm count tested. The preparation was well supported by all. Undesirable side effects were not observed in any of the patients.

The next paper, written in March 1966, reports on a joint Swedish-German study of 176 male patients in which twelve different urologists participated. The patients were suffering from a variety of sexual dysfunctions. The doctors who jointly authored the paper are C. E. Alken, M.D., professor of urology, Hamburg, Germany; G. Jonsson, M.D., head of the Urology Department, University Clinic, Lund, Sweden; and L. Rohl, M.D., associate professor of urology, Heidelberg, Germany. The patients were treated with an unidentified bee-pollen compound. According to the concluding remarks in the paper, "The number of sexual disturbances of any type occurring in these subjects was relatively high, i.e., 98 cases out of 176. Reduced libido, painful orgasm, premature ejaculation, and impotency occurred in about equal numbers. More than one of these symptoms of sexual dysfunction was present at the same time in many patients.

"A tabulation of results shows improvement averaged out at 44 percent. Given the wide variety of sexual dysfunctions treated, the improvement percentage is surprisingly high. No appreciable adverse side effects were observed."

A paper on a pollen compound used for a common prostate complaint comes from Sweden. Dr. Gosta Leander of Stockholm authored "A Memorandum Concerning a Statistical

Evaluation of the Results of a Clinical Investigation of Cernilton," which has been translated from the Swedish. (Cernilton is a Swedish grass-pollen preparation.) The men studied here were suffering from prostatovesiculitis, an inflammation of the seminal vesicles and prostate gland. Dr. Leander, reporting excellent results, says, "It can be confirmed that a statistical and highly significant effect of the compound could be demonstrated in prostatovesiculitis, estimated on the basis of a double-blind control study of 93 patients, 50 of whom received the compound and 43 of whom received the placebo. A 92 percent ascertained improvement was confirmed in the group given the compound. The effects of the compound determined during the course of this study have been established as statistically highly significant." In other words, forty-six men out of the fifty given the pollen compound were successfully treated. The inflammation and swelling of the prostate disappeared. In the control group given a placebo, no significant improvement was noted.

Interestingly enough, Dr. Leander went a step further with one of the patients. Simply put, he first gave this man a placebo with the expected results. Nothing happened. He then gave the man the pollen compound with the expected results. The prostatovesiculitis vanished. Dr. Leander says it this way: "A comparison of therapy results obtained for the same patient following, first, placebo, then the compound respectively, showed a statistical and highly significant effect from the compound." I like my way of putting it better.

A study at the University School of Medicine, Kyoto, Japan, provides yet more documentation regarding the beneficial effects of pollen on the prostate. An article on the study, "Use of Cernilton in Patients With Prostatic Hypertrophy," was published in *Acta Urologica Japonica* in June 1967. ("Prostatic hypertrophy" is a medical term for enlarged prostate.)

T. Inada, T. Kitagawa, and M. Miyakawa, who conducted the study, note in their article that this serious problem is on the rise in Japan. Most males over the age of seventy suffer from prostate problems. Some develop clinical symptoms that require treatment. One treatment for an enlarged prostate is the surgical removal of the gland, but surgery can be especially dangerous for older patients. Noninvasive treatment is preferred.

The three Japanese scientists report on twelve men with enlarged prostates who were treated at the outpatient clinic of the University School. Treatment consisted of administration of the pollen compound for periods ranging from one to five months. No other drugs were employed. According to the scientists, the study determined that "the pollen compound can be used effectively in cases where surgery is a risk or to improve clinical symptoms when the disease is still in its early phase. Side effects were observed in none of the cases treated with the pollen compound.

"Ten out of the twelve cases showed improvement. Of the ten men who improved, three were in the first stage of hypertrophy; four were in the second stage; and three were in the third and most serious stage of the condition. In two cases, symptoms recurred within one month after withdrawal of the drug. These patients eventually had their prostate glands removed surgically."

Are you wondering why the drug was withdrawn when improvement had been observed? So am I. Those patients who subsequently had their prostates removed are probably wondering, too. The Japanese doctors who conducted this study say, "It [the drug] should not be employed indiscriminately for long-term administration, as it may aggravate renal [kidney] function and thus increase the risk in surgical operations."

I am not privy to the Cernilton formula. It may be that the combination of chemical ingredients in the Cernilton pollen compound poses a medical risk over time. However, there are many studies that show bee pollen can be eaten regularly without risk. I have been eating great quantities of all the hive products every day for over twenty years.

What's that you say? I'm in my seventies and my prostate is functioning perfectly. Thank you for asking.

Another Japanese study of the same compound achieved measurably higher percentages of effectiveness. In an article published in 1967 in the *Japanese Journal of Clinical Urology*, researchers M. Ohkoshi, N. Kawamura, and I. Nagakubo review their results. Some of their statements are quite surprising. For example, they say that although prostate complaints are usually considered a problem that surfaces only as males become older, some authorities feel chronic prostatitis is found in more than 35 percent of males over the age of thirty-six. Other authorities, the researchers say, feel chronic prostatitis is found in 85 percent of males over the age of thirty. In most cases, the authorities apparently report that bacteria are either totally absent or only sparsely detected. If bacteria are not the cause of the inflammation, antibiotics are not effective. And long-term administration of anti-inflammatory drugs does not always bring improvement.

In the Japanese study, thirty-eight men with chronic prostatitis were involved. Fifteen were given the pollen compound and ten were given a placebo. The subjects were all diagnosed on the basis of their symptoms and findings on palpation. Of the fifteen men given the compound, ten were judged effectively cured. In the others, the symptoms were judged partially reduced. In the placebo group, the results were much less favorable. No side effects were noted.

The three Japanese researchers close their paper by observing, "The rate of effectiveness was higher than 80 percent in the group given the pollen compound. This shows that there are cases [of chronic prostatitis] where the compound is indicated. This theory is supported by the significant differences registered in the cases where both the compound and placebos were employed."

Bee pollen contains a gonadotropic hormone very similar to the human pituitary hormone, gonadotropin, which functions as a sex-gland stimulant. Research conducted at the University of Sarajevo with a group of impotent men showed that more than half of those treated with bee pollen exhibited a dramatic improvement in the production of sperm, gained a higher level of self-confidence, and were able to perform better sexually after taking bee pollen for just one month.

It isn't only scientists who are documenting this effect either. Noel Johnson, a marathon runner in his nineties and the author of two inspiring autobiographies, *A Dud at 70—A Stud at 80* and *The Living Proof,* credits bee products with the full restoration of his manhood (see page 111). Vigorous and virile today, Johnson, always the gentleman, doesn't "kiss and tell." He says simply, "I derive special nutrients from bee pollen. It gives me the energy I need to engage in marathons . . . and other physical activities."

Several studies, including the following, explain why hormone-loaded bee products can be considered a documented aid to sexual prowess.

In their paper entitled "The Gonad Stimulating Potency of Date Palm Pollen Grains," originally published in the French scientific journal *Experientia* in October 1957, Egyptian scientists F. A. Soliman and A. Soliman report, "Several investigators have extracted estrogenic material from palm kernels and date pollen grains. Recently, a gonad-stimulating principle was extracted from pollens. The combined activity of the two hormones [gonadotropic and estrogenic] present in one gram of pollen is close to 10 I.U.'s [International Units]. When injected into immature male and female rats, it increased the weight of their gonads and activated them."

Will a translation of the translation help? Scientifically speaking, "gonad" refers to both the male sex glands (testes) and female sex glands (ovaries). "Gonadotropic material" includes gonadotropin, a hormone that stimulates the release of both estrogen, a female hormone, and progesterone, a male hormone. In medical practice, gonadotropin is used to treat some cases of undescended testicles. It can also help stimulate the ovary of an infertile woman to release an egg (ovum).

More work on the sex-gland stimulating properties of pollen comes from Romania in the form of a study by Drs. Salajan and Baltan on the influence of maize pollen on ovulation. This is an important study. In it, Drs. Salajan and Baltan obtained increased ovulation in hens, greater strength of organisms (hen eggs) during incubation, and improvement in the biological value of eggs produced by hens given maize pollen. Of course, probably no one reading this book is planning to rush to Romania and start a chicken farm. You probably think I'm straying far afield in reporting this study. Nothing could be further from the truth.

A woman who wishes for a child but is unable to conceive may well welcome a food that can increase ovulation, thereby improving her chances of becoming pregnant. A woman planning to bear a child may well be interested in the enhancement of incubation values that bee pollen offers, even though she "incubates" her fetus in the womb, not in a mechanical device. And this same woman may well praise bee pollen on finding that the "biological value" of an egg (or a baby) can improve when the diet of the mother (hen or human) includes the powerful natural hormones and complete nutrition of bee pollen.

The Romanian paper is very long and I'm not going to ask you to wade through all the scientific protocols necessary to set up the experiment. Instead, I'm just going to tell you that the researchers took great care to insure all the factors were equal. For example, the hens were artificially inseminated using sperm from four brother roosters, all of whom had their sperm tested for quality. The sperm from the four fathers-to-be was mixed together, and the fertilization of all the hens, divided into six groups, was carried out immediately after the sperm was collected. The researchers came to the following conclusions:

> Pollen stimulates ovarian function. The best results were obtained with a pollen supplementation of 2 parts per 100 in the ration, and with the substitution of animal proteins with pollen in a proportion of 5 parts per 100. The intensity of ovulation increased.
>
> Parallel to this increase in ovulation, pollen also improves the ability of eggs to withstand the incubation period. The best results were obtained with a quantity of 4 parts per 100 of pollen added to the ration, resulting in an increase in the percentage of eggs in respect to the control group. The application of pollen is recommended whenever the end result is obtaining eggs for reproduction.

Pollen also exercises a positive influence on the nutritive quality of eggs. It increases the consumable proportion of the egg, its content of dry matter, the biological value and degree of pigmentation of the yolk. From this viewpoint, an optimum quantity of 2 parts per 100 of pollen is proposed. It is recommended that pollen be added to the rations during the growth period, and also during laying, which will increase ovulation and also improve the nutritive qualities of the eggs destined for consumption.

Other scientists agree with the Romanian findings. In translation from the German, the conclusion of an article on the same subject from the December 1983 issue of *Zeitschrift für Tierphysiologie, Tiernahrung und Füttermittelkunde (Periodical for Animal Physiology, Animal Nutrition and Fodder Science)* says, "Maize pollen is a powerful biostimulant that has positive action on the organism, including a gain of weight and the development of impressive bodily dimensions. Maximum stimulation is obtained with a dosage of 2 percent [by weight] of pollen. Further administration does not lead to an increase of weight but does have positive effects on sexual activity, notably the production of eggs."

Because this paper mentions weight gain, a subject of concern for many, it seems appropriate to add an explanatory note here. Since bee pollen synergistically boosts the nutritive value of food, cravings are eliminated and appetite is reduced, which means you automatically eat less. This phenomenon has been documented in many of the studies discussed in this chapter. By providing the body with all the natural elements it requires for the internal processing of each individual nutrient, bee pollen makes it easier for the body to extract and assimilate what it needs. Bee pollen will not add to a weight problem. Put that worry out of your mind for the moment. In fact, a little further along in this chapter, you'll discover why bee pollen has a place in a program for weight *loss*.

Now back to the subject at hand.

In translation from the Slavic, the next paper, by L. Pokrajcic and I. Osmanagic, is entitled "The Treatment With Melbrosin of Dysmenorrhea in Adolescence." (Melbrosin is the European bee-pollen-and-royal-jelly compound discussed on page 49. "Dysmenorrhea" is a medical term covering a wide range of menstrual problems.) The authors of this paper are physicians who practiced in a Yugoslavian gynecology clinic. Their study involved the treatment of young women suffering from menstrual problems, including premenstrual syndrome (PMS). In their opening remarks, the doctors particularly note that pain killers, tranquilizers, hormones, antispasmodics, and drugs are not always effective against menstrual disturbances.

The study included 120 girls between the ages of fifteen and twenty years, divided at random into two groups. Symptoms included pain in the abdomen before, at the beginning of, or during the entire period of menstruation. In some girls, the pain manifested as a spasm rising and falling in intensity. In others, the pain was constant. The localized abdominal pain was often accompanied by general symptoms, including headache, swelling and bloating, vomiting, insomnia, and depression. In some cases, the pain was so severe that the patients had to stay in bed throughout menstruation.

The administration of the bee-pollen-and-royal-jelly compound was very effective. According to the report's conclusion:

Following the ingestion of the compound during two full menstrual cycles, symptoms improved in almost all patients. Symptoms persisted in only five cases out of the sixty girls given the compound. Such obvious results of this therapy were assessed as being very good. In the control group not given the compound, only two girls of the sixty reported any symptomatic changes.

The positive effects of this preparation are due to the effects of the herbal hormones contained in the bee pollen and royal jelly. The compound may be administered for a long time. It is easily tolerated and does not give rise to undesired side effects.

For the first time in our country, we treated painful menstruation and dysmenorrhea in young women with a natural preparation of bee pollen and royal jelly. Encouraged by the results of this experiment, we have decided to initiate a thorough clinical testing of the compound in girls with difficult menses.

Focusing on the other end of a woman's menstrual life, Dr. Izet Osmanagic also carried out a study on the effects of the same bee-pollen-and-royal-jelly compound on women suffering problems with menopause. This study was conducted under the auspices of the Endocrinological Department of the University Clinic for Women at the Medical Faculty in Sarajevo. Osmanagic discusses his findings in his May 1972 report, "A Clinical Testing of the Effect of Melbrosin on Women Suffering From Climacteric Syndrome." ("Climacteric syndrome" is a medical term for menopause.)

In Osmanagic's study, all the patients were under treatment for menopausal complaints. Their ages ranged from thirty to sixty years, with the majority of patients being forty to fifty years old. The cases were divided into two groups. In the first group, menopause had occurred artificially. The ovaries of some of the women had been surgically removed, usually because of cancer. In others, radiation therapy had destroyed the ovaries. The women in the second group had passed through normal menopause. Here's what Osmanagic reports:

Results were particularly favorable in patients thrown into menopause by surgery or radiation treatment. The patients treated with radiation had especially serious complaints. An additional factor was that their hormones were depleted, probably by damage caused to the liver and blood-forming processes as a result of irradiation.

We proved that the compound exerts a beneficial effect throughout the whole system affected by radiation. Thanks to the therapeutic action of the compound, these women have experienced a general improvement in their condition. They feel fresher, more dynamic, open to every activity, and mentally calmer. The compound is easily taken and rarely causes side effects. The beneficial effects of the preparation are noticeable after only 14 days of treatment.

In our nomenclature, a good effect was achieved when symptoms had either completely disappeared after therapy or had significantly decreased both in number and degree. In the majority of patients (90 percent), we were able to assess more or less excellent positive results of treatment.

This study shows that the preparation should be used in the treatment of all patients subjected to irradiation, as well as in the treatment of patients suffering from all menopausal disturbances.

In general, all the studies discussed in this chapter show that bee pollen alone or in combination can be a tremendous help in the treatment of a wide variety of reproductive and sexual problems.

BEE PRODUCTS VERSUS ALLERGIES

Bee pollen and raw, pollen-rich honey have been effectively used down through the ages to rid allergy sufferers of their afflictions. This technique, called desensitization, was developed at St. Mary's Hospital Medical School in London soon after the turn of the century. The treatment consists of administering small amounts of the allergen to stimulate the patient's own immune system to produce antibodies that will eliminate the allergic reaction. It works rather like a vaccination does against childhood diseases. Desensitization is based on the premise that the administration of the allergen will cause the body to produce antibodies that will cancel out the effects of the offending substance when the patient is again exposed to it.

In the not-too-distant past, honey was administered by Great-grandmother as a treatment for many minor ills, including allergies, with great success. Modern science has determined that the active substance in the raw honey fresh from the beehive on which Great-grandmother relied is the microscopic pollen spore.

A British physician by the name of Gordon Latto rediscovered this old remedy and now successfully treats his hayfever patients with his own unfiltered, pollen-laden honey. He

reports that attacks are reduced during the first year of treatment. During the second year of treatment, Dr. Latto says, his
patients are entirely free of hay-fever symptoms.

Leo Conway, M.D., of Denver Colorado, went one better. He
treated his patients directly with pollen itself. Dr. Conway
reported:

> All patients who had taken the antigen [pollen] for three
> years remained free from all allergy symptoms, no matter
> where they lived and regardless of diet. Control has been
> achieved in 100 percent of my earlier cases and the field is
> ever-expanding.
>
> Since oral feeding of pollen for this use was first per-
> fected in my laboratory, astounding results have been
> obtained. No ill consequences have resulted. Ninety-four
> percent of all my patients were completely free from al-
> lergy symptoms. Of the other six percent, not one followed
> directions, but even this small percentage were nonethe-
> less partially relieved.
>
> Relief of hay fever, pollen-induced asthma, with ever-
> increasing control of bronchitis, ulcers of the digestive
> tract, colitis, migraine headaches, and urinary disorders
> were all totally successful.

Unfortunately, Dr. Conway, an early pioneer in the field of
allergies, is now deceased.

However, all around the world, clinical trials on the use of
the products of the beehive against allergies are on the increase.
Closer to home, my own company has also mounted some
trials. First, I'll give you some background. Then, I'll let you in
on the amazing results.

Since the early 1980s, my company has marketed a tableted
bee-pollen formula for allergies. Judging from the response we
have had, this product has brought amazing relief to many
allergy and asthma sufferers. In late 1990, we decided to document the effects of this formula in action, live, on camera.

In preparation for a company-sponsored thirty-minute television program, called an infomercial in the trade, we adver-

tised locally in the greater Phoenix, Arizona, metropolitan area for allergy and asthma sufferers. The relatively clear air of Arizona is reputed to be a safe haven for allergy sufferers, so we were not sure exactly how many people we might find. Many, many people responded.

After initial interviews, we invited a number of people to take our tablets on camera. In order to give our formula the most rigorous testing possible, we selected people whose symptoms were very strong, people who had been afflicted with allergies or asthma for many years. We deliberately took people who had not found adequate relief through prescribed medication, allergy shots, or over-the-counter preparations. We were not looking for an "edge." We wanted to try our compound formula on the toughest cases.

Once the allergy sufferers had been selected and agreed to participate in our trials on camera, we armed them with a stopwatch and started the cameras rolling. We asked our trial subjects to take a series of the tablets, called Formula X66 for purposes of the program, while chatting with us. The subjects were instructed to start the stopwatch when they took the first tablet and stop it when they felt relief. While we were waiting for the formula to take effect, we asked them to tell us all about their allergy and asthma symptoms.

If you ever have a chance to see this thirty-minute program, you'll be as amazed as we were. We knew, of course, that our allergy tablet was effective. What we did not know was just how lightning-fast it could bring relief. It actually eliminated long-standing symptoms in minutes. Everything from asthma to allergies to sinus problems cleared. These trials confirmed that bee pollen is wonderfully effective against a very wide range of respiratory distress.

In order to generate some truly scientific-based data, my company is now in correspondence with independent research labs. Our aim is to persuade one of the great medical teaching institutions to engage in true double-blind studies of our formula. Our on-camera results were impressive, but we know only solid clinical studies will cause the medical establishment to take notice.

BEE PRODUCTS AND PHYSICAL ACTIVITY

If there's one thing health authorities all over the world agree upon, it's the basic need to provide the body with some form of regular exercise as well as basic, whole nutrients. In fact, scientists say that for every 200 hours we spend exercising, we gain an additional year of life. They are talking about active, quality time, too—not an additional year spent feeble and bedridden.

A two-year study conducted by former Russian Olympic coach Remi Korchemny when he was coaching the track team at Pratt Institute in New York gives much insight into the part bee pollen can play in an active lifestyle. This double-blind study fulfilled all the criteria of scientific research. Korchemny's findings finally gave us a solid foundation for the dynamic effects reported by athletes taking bee pollen. What this study confirmed is that bee pollen actually does improve crucial recovery power after stressed performance. The runners Korchemny provided with bee pollen not only bettered their time in a second run around the track right after a full-out effort, but their bodies also quickly recovered their normal heart rate and blood pressure, and the athletes were ready to go again sooner. The team members taking the placebo couldn't keep up.

British author and nutritionist Dr. Maurice Hanssen says, "I look on pollen as being part of the athlete's ideal diet. I define the ideal athlete's diet as that diet which produces maximum performance when it is required, with no long-term harmful side effects. Your body is continually being renewed in the average half-life, which is the time taken for half your cells to be replaced. Protein, for example, is in the body for 80 days, but the time differs in different tissues. Blood serum, heart, liver, and kidneys are all 10 days, while bone, skin, and muscle are 158 days.

"The extraordinary richness of pollen in micro-elements cannot be stressed too much. We just cannot be sure that a normal diet produces enough in available forms, but the absorption properties of pollen allow the trace elements to be incorporated into the body structure without excessive loss."

The British Sports Council recorded increases in strength of as high as 40 to 50 percent in those taking bee pollen regularly. Even more astounding, the British Royal Society has reported height increases in adults who take pollen.

Antii Lananaki, coach of the Finnish track team that swept the Olympics in 1972, revealed, "Most of our athletes take pollen food supplements. Our studies show it significantly improves their performance. There have been no negative results since we have been supplying pollen to our athletes."

Alex Woodly, then executive director of the prestigious Education Athletic Club in Philadelphia, said, "Bee pollen works, and it works perfectly. Pollen allows super-stars to increase their strength and stamina up to 25 percent. This increase in strength and endurance may be the key to the secret regenerative power of bee pollen. Bee pollen causes a definite decrease in pulse rate. The whole beauty of bee pollen is that it's as natural as you can get. No chemicals. No steroids."

Renowned German naturalist Francis Huber was a great proponent of this miraculous food from the hive. Huber called bee pollen "the greatest body builder on Earth."

BEE POLLEN AND WEIGHT CONTROL

Bee pollen works wonders in a weight-control or weight-stabilization regimen by correcting a possible chemical imbalance in body metabolism that may be involved in either abnormal weight gain or loss. The normalizing and stabilizing effects of this perfect food from the bees are phenomenal.

In weight-loss programs, bee pollen stimulates the metabolic processes. It speeds caloric burn by lighting and stoking the metabolic fires. Honeybee pollen is coming to be recognized as Nature's true weight-loss food.

Bee pollen is a low-calorie food. It contains only ninety calories per ounce. (An ounce is about two heaping tablespoons.) It offers 15 percent lecithin by volume. Lecithin is a substance that helps dissolve and flush fat from the body. This is one reason why bee pollen lowers low-density lipoproteins (LDL) surer and faster than any other food while helping increase the

The Most Famous Bee-Pollen Fan in the World

It was 1961 when Ronald Reagan first learned about the benefits of bee pollen from Marjorie McCormick, author of The Golden Pollen. *While touring the country for the United States Chamber of Commerce, Reagan met McCormick. She gave him a copy of her book and some bee-pollen bars. In a handwritten thank-you note to her, Reagan said, "I was plowing a ranch paddock and by late afternoon, I was exhausted. Then I realized I had one of the bee pollen bars in my pocket. I ate it and swear it was not my imagination, but twenty minutes or so later, I was definitely conscious I was no longer fatigued and the chill I'd been feeling was gone." It is clear Ronald Reagan was personally convinced of the worth of bee pollen. He's been eating it regularly for over thirty years now.*

A phone call from Air Force One let my company know just how much President Reagan liked the bee-pollen bars called the President's Lunch Bars that we had formulated in his honor. We had been shipping both fresh bee pollen and the bars to the White House for some time, but one day, the steward of Air Force One called my office. He said that President Reagan had asked for the President's Lunch Bars on his last flight but that none were on board. "I want to make sure that never happens again," he said. We were happy to oblige. From that time forward, we shipped directly to the Steward's Office at Andrews Air Force Base, where Air Force One is hangared.

During President Reagan's visit to Japan in 1983, our bee-pollen bars were prominently displayed during a state luncheon in Tokyo. Both President Reagan and Prime Minister Nakasone munched on bars while the television cameras rolled. This caught the fancy of the Japanese media. I was delighted to read several accounts of this occurrence in newspapers. A translated excerpt from one article has this to say: "At the meeting, there was a conversation about Japanese food. Mr. Reagan and Mr. Nakasone both stated they were very much interested in healthy food. Mr. Nakasone is a bean lover and Mr. Reagan is a bee-pollen lover."

President Ronald Reagan

Ronald Reagan was still our president-elect when the first article appeared about his fondness for bee pollen. That article, entitled "Presidential Bee Power," was in the Natural Foods Business Journal *in January 1981. This was just the beginning. The fact that the United States had a president who followed a healthy lifestyle didn't escape the notice of the press. Unless it was strictly a hard-news story, many of the articles written about President Reagan included a mention of his bee-pollen preference.*

By the spring of 1984, President Reagan's fit lifestyle was so well known that Time *sent a reporter to our offices to check out the facts. Before giving any information to the press about our most famous client, we phoned the White House for permission to talk with the reporter. Permission was granted to confirm that we regularly shipped both fresh granules and bars to the First Family. Time subsequently ran an article entitled "Presidential Pollen" in its April 30, 1984, issue. Who says Time doesn't have a sense of humor? The accompanying picture showed a honeybee in place of the usual eagle on the Great Seal of the United States!*

Whether you are a Republican or Democrat, an admirer or detractor, approve wholeheartedly of the way President Reagan ran the country or were happy to see him leave office, doesn't matter one whit.

You can't deny Ronald Reagan remains a fine figure of a man yet today, in his eighties. This is a guy who held down the toughest job in the galaxy for eight years. (Research shows the regular use of bee pollen builds stamina.) Think about how fast he got back in the Oval Office after being shot in the chest on March 30, 1981. Remember how quickly he bounced back after undergoing major surgery on July 13, 1985. (Studies show the regular use of bee pollen heightens the body's powers of recovery.) All those nasty rumors that his hair is dyed have been refuted. (There are empirical reports from many delighted regular bee-pollen users who have recovered their normal hair color.) And how many times have you seen an active, hale, and hearty Ronald Reagan riding a horse, clearing brush, or chopping wood down on the ranch?

Ronald Reagan is no slouch. In the physical fitness and longevity sweepstakes, research shows quality bee pollen does make a difference. Ronald Reagan is living proof. There's no doubt his healthy lifestyle is a contributing factor. I like to think bee pollen helped.

helpful high-density lipoproteins (HDL), which science says protect against cholesterol and heart disease.

By boosting the value of each nutrient present in the food you eat, bee pollen also eliminates cravings. Its natural phenylalanine content acts as an appetite suppressant. Phenylalanine is a natural amino acid that the body requires. It acts on your appestat, the control center that signals fullness and hunger. Mother Nature knows what she's about. You just plain won't want to eat as much when you take bee pollen regularly. When you are overweight, phenylalanine exerts a natural appetite-suppressant effect. When you need to gain weight, the phenylalanine in bee pollen works in reverse.

The chemical drug in over-the-counter weight-loss products is a manmade cousin of phenylalanine called phenylpropanolamine. Phenylpropanolamine chemically depresses the appetite whether you are fat, thin, or just right. It can also give you the jitters and leave you with a drug-induced "hangover." Additionally, it can be addictive. Phenylpropanolamine is a common ingredient in many decongestants, explaining why one of the side effects of these products is loss of appetite. Products that include phenylpropanolamine as an ingredient must by law carry a warning that they should not be taken by persons with certain conditions, including thyroid problems and high blood pressure.

HEALTH AND BEAUTY

Basic beauty begins with the glow of good health, which shines from within. A scrubbed and radiant complexion transforms any woman (or man) into a singularly attractive person. On the other hand, dull, muddy skin, often caused by poor nutrition or personal hygiene, can detract from even the most attractive. Studies have shown that unhealthy or aging skin can be dramatically improved by the consumption of honeybee pollen.

When bee pollen is included daily in the diet, it not only gives you the glow of health and aids in safe, permanent weight loss, but it can also be blended into seemingly "magic potions" to smooth, soothe, and rejuvenate every inch of the outside of your body. Several relatively inexpensive mixtures of hive products, used externally, can revitalize and rejuvenate the complexion and may even eliminate acne.

Dr. Lars-Erik Essen, a dermatologist in Halsinborg, Sweden, pioneered the use of bee products for skin conditions. He treated many of his patients successfully for acne. Dr. Essen says, "Through transcutaneous nutrition, bee pollen exerts a profound biological effect. It seems to prevent premature aging of the cells and stimulates growth of new skin tissue. It offers effective protection against dehydration and injects new life into dry cells. It smooths away wrinkles and stimulates a life-giving blood supply to all skin cells.

"The skin becomes younger looking, less vulnerable to wrinkles, smoother, and healthier with the use of honeybee pollen," Dr. Essen says. "Taken internally or used externally, bee pollen exercises a suppressive effect on facial acne. It is also an important skin rejuvenator, primarily because it contains a high concentration of the nucleic acids RNA and DNA as well as a natural antibiotic factor."

The French, long noted for their preoccupation with all things beautiful, have done a great deal of research on the use of bee pollen and other hive products in cosmetic preparations. Dr. M. Esperrois of the French Institute of Chemistry notes that honeybee pollen contains potent antibiotics that can act to reverse the effects normal aging exerts on skin, correcting darkening, wrinkles, and blemishes.

Noted French beauty expert Count Michael d'Ornand also researched the products of the beehive. His studies led him to the conviction that aging of the skin, darkening, wrinkles, and blemishes can be successfully treated with specialized preparations that employ the bee's products. The Count points with pride to the "firsts" he personally created, some of which are still causing a stir in the cosmetic world. Count d'Ornand pioneered the use of chicken embryos as a skin-renewing agent and was the first to use royal jelly as an ingredient in luxurious skin-care products. The wondrous effects of royal jelly on the skin led to his research and subsequent use of bee pollen as well.

Professors N. Mankovsky and D. G. Chebotarev, two Russian scientists, confirm honeybee pollen stimulates cell renewal. They say, "The rejuvenation of skin and body cells can be encouraged by the administration of the poly-vitamins, microelements, enzymes, hormones, and amino acids present in bee pollen. These nutrients are needed by the body to form new tissue." These professors go on to praise the properties of bee pollen, calling them "vital to a form of internal and external rejuvenation at the cellular level."

Mother was wrong. Beauty isn't only skin deep. Proper attention to good nutrition and health practices will do more than just keep the doctor away. Vibrant health imparts a glow no cosmetic preparation can manufacture. The eighteenth-century poet William Shenstone said it best: "Health is beauty, and the most perfect health is the most perfect beauty."

LONGEVITY AND THE AGING PROCESS

Ponce de León didn't have to travel halfway around the world. He might have found what he was looking for in his own backyard if he had been a beekeeper. The products of the beehive have been used as both beautifiers and food since the dawn of time—and just might qualify as the legendary Fountain of Youth fabled in song and story.

In Norse mythology, the secret of the eternal life of the many gods was reputed to be ambrosia. Back then, ambrosia was simply an incredibly rich combination of raw honey and bee bread, another name for the bee pollen that bees store in the waxen cells of honeycomb. This same food was reserved for the original Olympic athletes of ancient Greece to increase their energy and enhance their performances. Ancient texts unearthed in Babylon, China, Persia, and Egypt agree this revered food contains the secret of eternal youth and health.

According to G. Liebold, a holistic physician and psychologist of Karlsruhe, Germany, "Bee pollen is an excellent prophylaxis and therapeutic treatment against all the precocious symptoms of old age. It should be considered a universal geriatric treatment in the form of a natural remedy.

"Bee pollen causes an increase in physical and mental abilities, especially of concentration and memory ability, activates sluggish metabolic functions, and strengthens the cardiovascular and respiratory systems. This natural nutriment from the bees removes the causes of cardiovascular symptoms, such as arteriosclerosis, cerebral insufficiency, and other sequelae. It prevents nutrient deficiency during old age, gravidity [pregnancy], and the lactation [nursing] period. Bee pollen accelerates convalescence after serious illness and/or an operation, increases the body's physical defensive powers of the immune system, stimulates mental and psychological resistance to stress, and creates a harmonizing of vegetative and hormonal disorders."

Dr. Nicolai Vasilievich Tsitsin, the USSR's chief biologist (and botanist) and an acknowledged expert on geriatrics, spent quite a few years pursuing the secrets of the many in what was the Soviet Union who live extraordinarily long lives. He visited the numerous small villages that dot the landscape high up in the Caucasus mountains, where the air is always clear and sweet. In summer, the breezes there are perfumed with the scent of thousands of wild flowers. The villagers work their small farms and tend their kitchen gardens without the dubious "benefits" of the space-age technologies employed by agribiz conglomerates. This is one of the few areas left in the world where the old ways still prevail.

The stalwart families who make their homes in the mountainous regions of the former Soviet Union are some of the most long-lived people in the world. On examination, many exhibit signs of "silent" heart disease, scars of "silent" heart attacks that would have almost certainly been lethal to a modern man or woman. The hard physical work they do every day well into what some of us in the so-called civilized world consider old age plays a part in their remarkably healthy lifestyle.

Dr. Tsitsin was amazed to find more than 200 individuals over 125 years of age, all still working every day and participating actively in village life. The hard facts of their daily existence partially explained the extended life span they achieved, but Dr. Tsitsin remained puzzled. He knew there had to be some other factor entering into the equation. He set himself the task of finding the common denominator. Then he stumbled upon it.

These people kept bees. Beekeeping is a profession that in itself historically confers some sort of "magical" life protection on its members, a fact validated by today's scientific research. Still, only very well informed, modern beekeepers are knowledgeable about the many health-promoting benefits of bee pollen and regularly serve it at table. The villagers didn't fit the profile. Dr. Tsitsin dug deeper.

He found the answer. These beekeepers, happy and fulfilled though they were with their almost idyllic pastoral existence, were very poor. Bartering among themselves to exchange homegrown or handmade products for services was the accepted way of life. They had little cash available to them, so they regularly harvested—and either sold or bartered away—the pure, clear honey from the combs of their beehives. What they kept for themselves and ate regularly was the thick residue that accumulated on the bottoms of their hives.

When he was served some of the sweet, sticky stuff in the home of one of the villagers, Dr. Tsitsin realized that this was the magic elixir that contributed to the remarkable longevity. The tasty but unattractive glob was rich with golden granules of bee pollen.

Dr. Tsitsin attributed the remarkable health and extended life spans of these particular Russians to the scientifically documented action of bee pollen. He concluded his report by saying, "Taken regularly and in sufficient amounts, bee pollen will prolong the life span of man for many years."

Another Russian scientist, Naum Petrovich Ioyrish, chief of the Academy of Vladivostok and author of *Bees and People,* agrees. In 1975, Dr. Ioyrish reported without any qualification, "Long lives are attained by bee pollen users. It is one of the original treasure houses of nutrition and medicine. Each grain contains every important substance necessary to life."

As one of Nature's nutritive storehouses, bee pollen qualifies as a dynamic vitamin-mineral-and-more supplement. Whether you are interested in putting these golden granules on your menu as a wholesome, whole food or as a natural preventive medicine, the best place for you to find this gift from the bees is your local health-food store.

SHOPPING FOR BEE POLLEN

Bee pollen is available fresh, canned, tableted, or capsulized. You'll also find it used as an ingredient in many all-natural formulas targeting specific conditions.

In order to keep them sweet tasting, fresh raw bee-pollen granules must be refrigerated. Each little granule contains a multitude of live pollen spores, tightly packed and tamped together by the bee that collected them. Fresh granules are usually slightly dried to remove excess moisture. The moisture removal consists of sending a controlled flow of dry air over a tray of granules for a short time. High heat is a no-no. Too much heat destroys the nutrients and actually "kills" the pollen spores. Fresh granules are available in sealed poly bags in weights ranging from one-half pound to five pounds. Look for fresh bee-pollen granules in the refrigerator case of your favorite health-food store.

Many producers offer canned bee pollen in half-pound and one-pound containers. Canned bee pollen also consists of fresh granules that have been slightly dried to remove excess moisture. Before the can is sealed, nitrogen is pumped in to force the damaging oxygen out. To make sure you're getting a quality product, look for canned bee pollen marked "nitrogen packed."

When shopping for bee pollen in tablet or capsule form, it's very important to make sure the source is reliable. If the label does not state the origin of the bee pollen, it is probably an inexpensive, single-source import. You won't be able to tell if the bee pollen in the finished product is good, bad, or indifferent after it has been ground up and mixed in with the tableting or capsulizing ingredients.

Single-source bee pollens just cannot contain all the nutrients Nature intended. There's a very good reason for this. One of the most disturbing facts I uncovered while researching bee products is that there is not one area left in the United States—perhaps in the entire world—where the soil still contains a complete complement of nutrients. This fact is substantiated by the soil-nutrient profiles of each state within the United States. It took me three and a half years of intensive research to gather these soil studies together. I consulted every government source I could find, including the United States Department of Agriculture and many county extension agents. I wasn't at all pleased to realize that chemical fertilizers, pesticides, herbicides, soil enhancers, and so on were being used in alarming quantities to try to correct the soil deficiencies people had caused in the first place.

Once I had the soil profiles from every state, I laboriously consolidated and extensively analyzed the mountain of information. What I found was frightening. Thanks to human tinkering with the environment, there is not one state left where the soil still has all the nutrients present that should be there.

If the nutrients are not in the soil, they can't be in the pollen the bees gather from the plants growing in that soil. What this means is that pollens are top heavy in some nutrients, deficient in others. For example, high concentrations of selenium are found in North and South Dakota and in some parts of Colorado, New Mexico, and Arizona. However, the entire northern portion of the United States from Washington and Oregon to New England—the area that was once covered by glaciers, which left tons of nutrients in their wake—along with the East Coast and most of California have soils *deficient* in many minerals, including zinc and iodine, and all the water-soluble vitamins. States on the East Coast and in the Midwest are universally deficient in many trace elements, including selenium, one of the important minerals science says protects the heart. The soils in these states also test very low for the water-soluble vitamins, including all the B vitamins and ascorbic acid (vitamin C).

Here's a big surprise: citrus fruits grown in California, the Golden State, contain 50 percent *less* vitamin C than citrus grown in Texas and Florida. The soils of California test the lowest of all the fifty states in calcium. However, the California climate offers something no other state can match. California has eucalyptus trees that live a thousand years.

I had to conclude that only a true multisource bee pollen can really be called Nature's perfect food. It was certainly apparent to me that the only way to deliver the "best bee pollen" in the world was to blend pollens from many areas. I really didn't want to go to the trouble and expense of mixing pollens harvested in so many different areas. Why? This is a very costly procedure. I realized the blending process would inevitably result in excessive powdering of the fragile granules, leading to the loss of a high percentage of the product. Still, blending was necessary. Once I knew about the soil deficiencies, I had to do my best.

It's manifestly impossible to shop for fresh foods on the basis of where they are grown. You can't very well go into a produce market and ask for one stalk of broccoli grown in Arizona (for its selenium), another grown in Florida (for its vitamin C), and another grown in Montana (for its trace minerals). Produce doesn't come with a label giving a nutrient breakdown. On the other hand, blended multisource bee pollen really does offer a full complement of Nature's nutrients.

When shopping for bee pollen, you don't have to be an expert to judge bee-pollen granules, be they fresh or canned. You can see, feel, and, best of all, taste the difference. Trust your senses.

See. Pour out a bit of fresh pollen and take a good look at it. Although most bee-pollen granules are varying shades of gold, a good multisource bee pollen will exhibit a mixture of colors. These colors can range from a very pale straw shade all the way across the spectrum through orange, brown, and purple to almost black. Occasionally, some pure reds and beautiful blues show up. Treasure these rarities.

Feel. Roll a granule around. It should be a little soft and springy. Rock-hard grains have most likely been subjected to high heat. Too much heat kills live enzymes, reduces nutrient content. If your bee pollen crunches between your teeth, you can be pretty sure most of the live nutrients and all the vital enzymes have been destroyed in the processing.

Taste. The proof of the pollen is in the eating. Although some high heat treated pollens taste rather good, though very hard and crunchy, you might as well eat potato chips for all the nutrient value they offer. Worse, a lot of imported pollens, even some harvested here at home, are chewy, gummy, and musty tasting. Stale pollen grains are unpalatable. They taste just plain nasty. Even some nitrogen-canned bee pollens have this telltale taste. If they go into the can old and stale, all the nitrogen flushing in the world won't make them taste good.

But fresh raw bee-pollen granules taste the way flowers smell: faintly sweet and as field-fresh as a sunny meadow filled with spring flowers dancing gently in a warm breeze. Think of chewing on a tender blade of grass or nibbling on a flower petal when you were a youngster and you'll come close.

HOW TO USE BEE POLLEN

It's difficult to pinpoint recommended dosages for bee pollen. Fresh (or nitrogen-flushed canned) bee pollen is the richest food in Nature. Each golden granule is densely packed with live enzymes and just about every nutrient that has a name, plus some elements that science has not yet identified and labeled. Your digestive system may not be accustomed to such intensely rich food.

I personally eat around two cupfuls of fresh granules every day, but I've been eating all the products of the beehive for more than twenty years. I also chew tablets flavored with honey and vanilla, and relish bee-pollen bars made with peanut butter and other whole ingredients. (See Chapter 8.)

If you are a beginner, introduce bee pollen into your diet slowly, a granule or two at a time. Whether you are beginning with granules, tablets, capsules, or a combination formula, follow the label directions.

Once you are accustomed to all the richness, there are many ways to enjoy the sweet-tart tasting granules. I eat them by the spoonful, but you may prefer to enjoy them in other ways. You can reduce the grains to powder by grinding them in a seed, nut, or coffee grinder. The resulting powder mixes with—and improves the nutrient value of—just about anything.

Just don't cook with the granules or add powdered granules to anything that requires heat. Heat destroys the live enzymes and reduces the nutrient value. Otherwise, the sky's the limit. Following are a few suggestions to get you started.

Powder an ounce or two of granules and add cinnamon to taste. Cinnamon adds a delightful spiciness and aroma to the sweetness of pollen. This mixture makes a tasty topping for applesauce or yogurt. Or enjoy it "as is," by the spoonful.

Stir powdered granules into vegetable or fruit juices, or even into water sweetened with raw honey. Whirl the powder into protein shakes and salad dressings. Sprinkle whole or powdered granules on toast topped with honey or peanut butter. Stir a spoonful into yogurt. Top off your morning bowl of cold whole-grain cereal with a sprinkle of Nature's sunshine.

The following two bee-pollen recipes come from my daughter. Both are favorites at home. My staff is particularly partial to the candy. When my daughter brings a batch to the office, it disappears in no time.

Honeybee Pollen Candy

½ cup bee-pollen granules
2 tablespoons carob powder
2 tablespoons water
3 tablespoons raw honey
½ cup crunchy peanut butter

1. Put the bee-pollen granules in a mixing bowl. Dissolve the powdered carob in the water and stir into the bee pollen.

2. Add the raw honey and mix.

3. Add the peanut butter and mix thoroughly.

4. Using a melon baller, form little balls from the mixture. Store the candy balls, which will remain soft, in the refrigerator.

Yield: 18 balls

Honeybee Pollen Milkshake

⅝ cup nonfat milk
½ cup ground bee pollen
¼ cup carob powder
¼ cup ground almonds

1. Place the nonfat milk in a blender. Add the powdered bee pollen and carob, and blend well.

2. Add the powdered almonds and blend thoroughly.

3. Pour the shake into a large glass and drink immediately.

Yield: 1 serving

If you like fooling around in the kitchen, you'll find ways of your own to enjoy bee pollen. A tasty and healthful confection can be made to suit your family's tastes by mincing and mixing granules with any of the following in pleasing proportions: dried apricots or other dried fruit, orange peel, raisins, dates, figs, coconut, seeds, nuts, and granola. Use your imagination. Bind the mixture together with a small amount of raw honey and drop by teaspoonfuls onto wax paper. Roll the balls in coconut, chopped nuts, or seeds, or coat them with melted carob. These snacks are both delicious and nutritious.

4

PROPOLIS

 The term "propolis" comes from two Greek words: "pro," which means "before," and "polis," which means "city." This ancient term came into being centuries ago when some early Greek student of Nature established the fact that honeybees use propolis to narrow the opening into their "cities," or hives, to keep out unwelcome intruders. Many sources attribute the word to Aristotle (384–322 B.C.).

WHAT IS PROPOLIS?

Propolis is the sticky resin that seeps from the buds of some trees and oozes from the bark of other trees, chiefly conifers. Bees seem to prefer poplar propolis. You might not notice propolis exuding from the new buds that plants put forth in season every year, but we've all seen shiny dribbles of resinous sap on the trunks of trees.

The bees gather propolis, sometimes called bee glue, and carry it home in their pollen baskets. They blend it with wax flakes secreted from special glands on their abdomens. In addition to using it to reduce the size of the hive entrance, bees also use this wax mixture as a caulking compound to plaster up any unwanted holes or openings to the outside.

Propolis is used to slickly line the interior of brood cells in preparation for the queen's laying of eggs, a most important procedure. With its antiseptic properties, this propolis lining insures a hospital-clean environment for the rearing of brood.

Propolis is also used to completely seal off any dead aliens that have somehow managed to penetrate the city's considerable defenses. A wasp or other foreigner that makes it inside the hive is immediately stung to death. If the intruder is too large for the housekeeping bees to remove, it is quickly covered with a thick layer of propolis, completely sealing it off and thus preserving the pristine cleanliness of the hive.

Unless they themselves harvest propolis for market, beekeepers find it a nuisance. Although it hardens in the cold, propolis remains soft and sticky during warm weather. It gets all over beekeepers' hands and clothes when they try to work a hive. Because bees instinctively close up any extraneous spaces inside the hive with propolis, a thick layer of the stuff is found around the edges of the comb. In order to harvest a full comb of honey, a beekeeper has to cut around the edges to free the comb before he can remove it from the hive.

On the other hand, migrating beekeepers who transport their hives long distances to pollinate agricultural crops appreciate the industry of the bees. The propolis caulking helps hold all the parts of the hives steady as they are bounced around when being trucked to distant fields.

PROPOLIS THROUGH THE AGES

Pliny the Elder (79–23 B.C.), the great Roman scholar, had much to say about this natural medicinal from the bees. Pliny's encyclopedic, thirty-seven-volume *Historia Naturalis* talks extensively of propolis, separating it into three distinct categories: "commosis," which refers to the bees' use of propolis as a disinfectant "paint" for brood cells and the interior of the hive; "pissoceros," the mixture of propolis and wax used to close holes and reinforce structurally weak areas; and "propolis," used to reduce the size of the entrance to the bees' "polis," or city. Pliny also identified the medicinal action of propolis, citing its abilities to reduce swelling, soothe pain, and heal the most hopeless sores.

Is propolis related to frankincense and myrrh, mentioned in the holy writings of many civilizations? Even theological scholars well versed in the intricacies of Biblical language aren't sure of the exact constituents of these legendary substances.

A modern dictionary tells us frankincense is an aromatic gum resin from various trees, chiefly used in perfumery and for burning as incense in ceremonial practices. Myrrh is defined as an aromatic resinous exudation from certain plants, also used chiefly in perfume and incense. What we don't know is how frankincense and myrrh were collected in Biblical times. Because both are resinous exudations, as is propolis, some authorities believe the ancients gathered these holy substances directly from the hives of wild bees.

In Matthew 2:11, we learn frankincense and myrrh were considered so precious in ancient times that, along with gold, they were carried as gifts to the newborn Christ Child. In Exodus 30:23–25, the Lord God instructs Moses in the preparation of "an ointment compounded after the art of the apothecary; it shall be a holy annointing oil." One of the principal components of this holy ointment is myrrh. In Exodus 30:34–38, the Lord God directs Moses, "thou shalt make perfume, a confection after the art of the apothecary, tempered together, pure and holy." This holy perfume employs frankincense. There are other Biblical references to these two holy substances as well.

The Koran mentions propolis and identifies it as being distinctly different from bee pollen. Before their destruction by the Spanish conquistadors, the Incas (circa 1600) used propolis topically against inflammations and swellings of all kinds. During the Boer War (1888–1902), propolis mixed with petroleum jelly was used to disinfect wounds sustained in battle and to speed healing. It worked, too.

On the technical side, propolis has long been the raw material of choice for the production of an exceptionally fine and smooth varnish. The famed Antonius Stradivarius (1644–1737) hand-mixed his own propolis varnish and used it to finish the incomparable musical instruments he handcrafted so long ago in his shop in Cremona, Italy. In his lifetime, Stradivarius produced only 1,116 stringed instruments. Those that survive, chiefly mellow-toned violins, are priceless. Musicians fortunate enough to possess one have said that a "Strad" plays itself. Stradivarius's formula for varnish has been lost. This may be one reason why the workmanship of this acknowledged master has never been duplicated.

Electromicroscopic analysis of a Guarnieri violin dating back to 1750 reveals the presence of bee pollen, bee hairs, and bits of propolis in the varnish. In 1961, German researchers Knopt and Ogait almost, but not quite, succeeded in producing a varnish identical in composition to the hand-mixed varnish used by Stradivarius and Guarnieri. String-instrument manufacturers in many countries still buy propolis regularly, presumably hoping to duplicate the magic Stradivarius instilled in his instruments.

In past centuries, propolis dissolved in alcohol was used to preserve the shining finish of the gold leaf that brightens statuary, moldings, and plaster ornamentation on walls and panels, fashionable at many times throughout history. Propolis dissolved in turpentine or alcohol was often added to molten silver or tin to give the resulting leaves and bars a rich golden hue. Leather treated with propolis develops a superior luster, which is why this process is still used in tanning today in some remote areas of the world.

In Mongolia and Siberia, natives often diluted propolis with oil or turpentine and immersed their sleds in the mixture. It is written that wood so treated is able to withstand the worst snow and cold without cracking or rotting. Propolis has always been in demand in Russia and other areas of the world where the weather is intensely cold.

THE PROPOLIS HUNTER

In spite of the importance of propolis to the colony, there are usually just a few propolis-gathering specialists in each hive. Bees of foraging age collect propolis only during warm days, when the resinous exudate is soft and malleable. The propolis hunter flies to the source, bites into it with her sharp mandibles, and tears off a tiny glob. If the source is exceptionally sticky, the bee may take time to knead the glob into shape before transferring it to one of her pollen baskets. She then repeats the procedure, placing the next bit into the pollen basket on her opposite leg. She continues this way, placing tiny globs in the baskets on alternate legs to keep her load balanced. If the source becomes exhausted and the bee must search for more, it may take an hour to complete the task.

Once her baskets are chock-full, the bee returns to the hive with her burden. There she is met by one or more receiving bees, whose task it is to help her unload. The helpers reverse the procedure, biting and pulling off one tiny piece of propolis at a time before mixing it

A hunter gathering propolis.

with wax and pressing it firmly into the area of the hive selected for reinforcement. Because the receiving bees may be busily secreting wax flakes and blending propolis into the flakes as they work, this unloading procedure can take several hours before the propolis hunter's baskets are completely empty. After the propolis hunter is free of her load, she flies off to forage for more propolis.

Science has established that bees are impervious to any virus or bacteria. This innate ability to defend themselves against infectious disease is very important. Any contagion could run rampant and rapidly destroy all 20,000 to 100,000 members of a colony living together in the very close quarters of a hive. Certainly the bees' good health can be attributed, at least in part, to a genetic immunity.

The bees are out and about in an increasingly polluted environment every day. They come in contact with many chemicals—most of which are harmful—in a day's work. But they enjoy yet another form of natural protection. The experts point out that bees are effectively "decontaminated" as they pass through the propolis barrier guarding the entrance to the hive.

THE CONSTITUENTS OF PROPOLIS

Chemically speaking, propolis is a very complex mixture. Its chemical elements vary according to its source. Colors range from golden brown to brownish green to reddish brown to blackish brown. A broad analysis reveals approximately 55 percent resinous compounds and balsam, 30 percent beeswax, 10 percent ethereal and aromatic oils, and 5 percent bee pollen. Many flavonols contribute to propolis. Other components include cinnamic acid, cinnamyl alcohol, vanillin, caffeic acid, tetochrysin, isalpinin, pinocembrin, chrysin, galangin, and ferulic acid.

THE PROPERTIES OF PROPOLIS

Propolis is another medicinal marvel from the beehive. Research shows it offers antiseptic, antibiotic, antibacterial, antifungal, and even antiviral properties. Propolis is Nature's premiere preventive. It is so powerful in action, it is often called Russian penicillin in acknowledgement of the extensive research the Russians have mounted on this wonder worker from the bees.

Propolis demonstrates strong antimicrobial properties against various bacterial and fungal infestations. Even streptococcus bacteria have been shown sensitive to propolis. The experts say that at least part of this documented bacteriostatic power can be attributed to the galangin, caffeic acid, and ferulic acid content of propolis.

For an overview of the many benefits of propolis, we turn to a paper entitled "Propolis, Natural Substance, the Way to Health," by naturalist and medical writer K. Lund Aagaard. In this eight-page paper translated from the Danish, Dr. Aagaard reports on extensive research conducted in Scandinavia.

Because Dr. Aagaard is so well respected in the European medical community, he was able to secure the cooperation of a vast number of his colleagues. This paper reports on the experimental use of propolis on more than 50,000 persons all across Scandinavia. Based on both the results he obtained using propolis on his own patients and the results obtained by his fellow physicians in thousands of additional cases, Dr. Aagaard has become a firm supporter of this natural substance from the beehive. He reached the following conclusions:

The field of influence of propolis is extremely broad. It includes cancer, infection of the urinary tract, swelling of the throat, gout, open wounds, sinus congestion, colds, influenza, bronchitis, gastritis, diseases of the ears, periodontal disease, intestinal infections, ulcers, eczema eruptions, pneumonia, arthritis, lung disease, stomach virus, headaches, Parkinson's disease, bile infections, sclerosis, circulation deficiencies, warts, conjunctivitis, and hoarseness.

Propolis helps regulate hormones and is an antibiotic substance that stimulates the natural resistance of the body. Propolis may be used by everyone, sick or healthy, as a means of protection against microorganisms. Propolis is also efficient against conditions caused by bacteria, viruses, or different fungi. Propolis cures many diseases because it is a special natural substance with strong effect.

The whole research program had a single purpose, namely, to investigate this substance against the great number of diseases mentioned. The numerous healings are relevant by themselves, and the number of people who use propolis is ever increasing.

In Romania, medical researchers N. Popovici and N. Oita zeroed in on one of the most important effects of propolis. Their paper is entitled "Influence of Extracts of Propolis on Mitosis." ("Mitosis" is a medical term for cell division, the process by which cells replicate themselves.) In cancer, malignant cells divide (and conquer) by multiplying wildly. Obviously, a substance that affects cell division is very important in the management of this lethal disease.

Earlier published reports of successful treatments using propolis against malignant tumors and leukemia were what led Drs. Popovici and Oita to mount their own study. The researchers note that it is not uncommon for the human body to harbor malignant cells. In the healthy body, the immune system destroys cancer cells regularly.

It is a medical fact that even when a tumor gets a toehold, tissue never becomes completely malignant. Cancer cells grow alongside normal cells. In time, malignant cells may become too numerous for the immune system to handle. Cancerous cells eventually can encroach on and crowd out normal cells. However, propolis appears to provide breathing space. Because propolis acts to hold back the growth of malignant cells while simultaneously boosting the activity of normal cells, it can actually give the body time to recoup and recover its normal healthy condition.

Drs. Popovici and Oita took note of numerous cancer patients treated with propolis whose tumors went into remission, as well as leukemia patients who were in remission after being given propolis. Although these early reports are certainly encouraging, the paper, translated from the original Romanian, concludes with a recommendation for additional study: "Further experiments are necessary to determine the relation between remissions of cancerous tumors and leukemia as a result of the administration of propolis, as well as the effects this bee product has on human cells."

In Chapter 3, we reported on one of the few studies conducted in the United States on the medicinal value of bee products. It confirmed the stunning cancer-fighting properties of bee pollen. This important work by Dr. William Robinson of the United States Department of Agriculture dates back to the late 1940s.

In 1991, over forty years later, the Comprehensive Cancer Center and Institute of Cancer Research of Columbia University mounted a study of the medicinal effects of another bee product, propolis. This study was on the "Suppression of Adenovirus Type 5 E1A-Mediated Transformation and Expression of the Transformed Phenotype by Caffeic Acid Phenethyl Ester (CAPE)." Whew! The name alone is enough to put you off. But remember, no drug known combats a virus. If you go to your doctor with a viral condition, you will be out of luck; all your doctor can offer you is symptomatic relief. This is why caffeic acid phenethyl ester (CAPE) promises to figure prominently in the future treatment of many conditions caused by viruses.

CAPE, directly extracted from bee propolis, has proven so effective against certain viral infections and some cancers that a United States patent was granted on April 16, 1991. Although the federal government retains an interest in the product, major interest in CAPE has been assigned to Columbia University, where the research continues.

Because the papers filed with the patent are so illuminating, the material that follows is drawn primarily from the data supporting the patent, which include reference to the subject study. The medical effects of propolis to which the data refer are well supported by parenthetical citations of previous authoritative studies of propolis. The Columbia University study documents the effectiveness of CAPE against both adenovirus (type 5 E1A) and a chemical-viral carcinogenesis in the form of a specific mouse mammary-tumor virus.

I'll spare you most of the scientific gobblydegook, but permit me a few excerpts. This first bit takes note of the use of propolis in history and its continued broad use across the ocean. It also remarks on the lack of side effects of natural medicines as compared to manmade drugs. Specifically, it says, "Propolis, a popular 'folk medicine' purported to have therapeutical benefit, is a brownish mass produced by honeybees. A significant number of so-called 'folk medicines' have withstood scientific scrutiny, with many of their purported therapeutic benefits being attributable to distinct chemical entities. Such naturally derived compounds often produce fewer and less serious side effects as compared to analogous man-made pharmaceuticals. . . . Propolis is alleged to exhibit a broad spectrum of activities. It is marketed in health stores as a natural antibiotic; aqueous extracts are sold in Europe as a cough syrup and sore throat remedy; compounds prepared from it are used to treat skin inflammations; ingestion of raw propolis is reputed to clear sinuses and treat viral infections; and propolis has been used to arrest the growth of tumors."

Remember the Romanian study that showed cancer patients treated with propolis went into remission? Columbia University sat up and took notice, too. According to the university's researchers, "The invention provides a method for substantially inhibiting the growth of transformed cells without substantially inhibiting the growth of normal cells. . . . The transformed cells may comprise carcinoma or melanoma cells. In the preferred embodiments, the subject is a human and the transformed cells are human carcinoma or melanoma cells, such as human breast carcinoma cells, colon carcinoma cells, renal carcinoma cells, or melanoma cells."

The researchers tested the propolis extract on human cancer cells. Although the cells were in a test tube, not in a living, breathing body, the results are conclusive. Because this data is so highly technical, I have "translated" the conclusion to this paper into more familiar terminology for you.

Basically, here's what happened when the scientists tested the effect of CAPE on human cancer cells in culture. They determined that 5 micrograms per milliliter (μg/ml) of CAPE inhibits the incorporation of transformed (cancerous) cells into the DNA of human breast cells by approximately 50 percent.

Blocking even half of the cancer cells was certainly spectacular, but then the scientists took the logical next step. By increasing the strength of the solution to 10 μg/ml, incorporation of the transformed cells was completely blocked. Similar inhibitions were observed for colon and kidney carcinoma cells. The effect of CAPE on normal cells was significantly less.

In the scientists' own words, here's the summing up of the Columbia University study: "Because the cytostatic action of CAPE is more dramatic on transformed cells, one may reasonably assume that it is at least partly responsible for the claimed carcinostatic (cancer-inhibiting) properties of propolis."

In brief, the patent granted for CAPE is based on how the product is extracted from propolis as well as on its effectiveness against cancer. The anti-inflammatory effects of the compound are also identified. The data that accompany the patent cite many previous studies supporting propolis's medicinal value.

What all this technical talk boils down to is this: CAPE, an extract of propolis, slows the growth and proliferation of "transformed" (cancer) cells without significantly damaging normal cells when it is administered in sufficient quantity.

The biggest problem medical science faces when trying to destroy diseased cells is that drugs powerful enough to kill diseased cells also unavoidably kill normal cells. The magic bullet the whole world is seeking is a selective substance that will attack and destroy only transformed, diseased cells while leaving normal cells unharmed. Perhaps CAPE, extracted from propolis, is that magic bullet.

Another very valuable property of the natural products of the beehive is that they exhibit true immunostimulating characteristics. Unlike many modern manmade drugs, beemade products do not depress the immune system. Instead, propolis (and bee pollen) actually boost the immune defense forces of the body.

The USSR conducted considerable research on propolis. In a paper entitled "Propolis Impact on the Immunogenesis in the Case of Immunization With Anatoxin," Soviet scientists V. P. Kivalkina and E. L. Budarkova documented the added effect propolis exerts on the immune system.

Like other published reports, this paper begins by citing

previous studies that show propolis stimulates the immunologic reaction. In order to prove it to themselves, the Russian researchers experimented on rabbits. One group was given an antitoxin alone; the other was given the antitoxin boosted with propolis. After being immunized, the animals were injected with diseased cells. According to the concluding statement, which has been translated from the Russian, "Our present work studies the effects of propolis on the immunologic rates by simultaneous administration with antitoxin. The experimental animals given antitoxin with propolis were protected from death to a greater extent than was the control group given antitoxin alone. The data we obtained demonstrate that the immunization of animals with propolis-antitoxin stimulates specific and nonspecific factors. As the antitoxin accumulated, the protective characteristics increased. We showed conclusively that the propolis-antitoxin protected the animals to a greater extent than the antitoxin alone."

Equally impressive results were obtained by V. P. Kivalkina, A. I. Balalykina, and V. I. Piontkovski. This paper, also translated from Russian, is entitled "Plasmocitary Response in White Mice Immunized With an Antigen Associated With Propolis." Except for the fact that these scientists used mice instead of rabbits, this study is a duplicate of the earlier work detailed above. This second study's conclusion says, "The response was 3.7 to 4 times greater in animals innoculated with the propolis-antigen than the response obtained in animals innoculated with the antigen alone or with the antigen combined with other additives. Cell analysis shows that the immunologic response is more intensely manifested in a very short time by the addition of propolis to the antigen. We conclude that propolis-antigens stimulate the immune response and speed up the development of antibodies." This second study reinforces the first Soviet study. Propolis boosts immune system functioning.

NATURE'S PREVENTIVE MEDICINE

Propolis has been justly called Nature's premiere preventive. The studies just discussed show why. The immune system is supported and strengthened by the ingestion of propolis. Modern scientific studies indicate that those who take propolis regularly escape winter colds and sore throats and seem to develop a natural immunity to common viruses, including the various strains of flu.

Chemical antibiotics destroy *all* bacteria in the body, both the friendly, necessary flora required for healthy functioning in the entire gastrointestinal tract and the bad intestinal flora. An individual who constantly takes prescribed antibiotics for one condition after another soon learns to his sorrow that the drugs may no longer work as well as they once did. As invading bacteria get "smarter," the drugs become less and less effective.

It is a medical fact that some biologically harmful strains of bacteria develop a resistance to chemical antibiotics. Some harmful microorganisms are able to subtly change their characteristics. Where once certain strains were easily destroyed by medical drugs, a bacteria can develop defensive characteristics that leave the body open to its destructive effects.

Propolis, the natural antibiotic, works against harmful bacteria without destroying the friendly bacteria the body needs. Propolis has also been proven effective against strains of bacteria that resist chemical antibiotics.

Perhaps you still doubt the antibiotic effects of propolis. If so, the following paper will change your mind. In it, Polish scientists S. Scheller, J. Tustanowski, and Z. Paradowski describe how they pitted propolis against some well-known antibiotics to find out which is more effective against the staphylococcus bacteria. The title, translated into English, is "Comparative Study on the Staphylococcus Sensitivity to Propolis and to Antibiotics."

You probably have a nodding acquaintance with "staph." It can cause all kinds of nasty symptoms, including nausea, vomiting, diarrhea, pus-forming abscesses, and pneumonia. A staph infection is a common secondary problem in many hospital patients. The bacteria are very difficult to combat. To make matters worse, there are many different varieties (strains) of staphylococcus.

In their opening remarks, the Polish scientists note that

The Infant Who Failed to Thrive

On August 31, 1982, a daughter was born to Emily and Clement A. Cox. With a five-year-old son, Joshua, at home, the Coxes were overjoyed with baby Colleen. Following the usual procedure, the delivery-room nurse rated Colleen's condition by the Apgar method. The newborn's heart rate, respiration, muscle tone, reflexes, and color were all judged excellent. Out of a possible ten, Colleen scored a very healthy nine.

When Colleen reached six months of age, Emily worried because the baby had not yet made an attempt to reach for a toy, hadn't yet rolled over. Colleen wasn't gaining the weight she should, her nails weren't growing, her hair was a sparse fuzz. Colleen seemed listless, didn't smile as often as she had earlier. When Emily voiced her fears at Colleen's six-month checkup, her pediatrician reassured her, saying babies develop at their own rate. When Colleen reached the eight-month mark and had made no progress, Emily and Clem again confronted Colleen's pediatrician. On his recommendation, they took Colleen to the Pediatric and Neurology Service at Yale–New Haven Hospital for testing and evaluation.

The diagnosis was cruel. It read, "This is a severely developmentally delayed floppy child whose differential includes a structural abnormality in the brain or a genetic abnormality, some of which may be diagnosed by chromosome analysis or genetic screen." Treatment was initiated immediately, but a week later, because Colleen was not responding, the Yale–New Haven doctors referred the child to the Easter Seals Foundation Rehabilitation Center.

The rehab center listed Colleen's condition as "severe receptive and expressive speech; language delay; immature neuromotor functioning; delay in development of play/cognitive skills; questionable hearing/acuity perception; severe delays in all areas of development; severe hypotonia." The prognosis was charted as "guarded due to yet unclear etiology. Positive prognostic signs, however, include the early age of intervention, plus parental support and motivation."

Easter Seals recommended a twice-weekly program, augmented by weekly participation in the Infant Stimulation program. In total, Colleen received more than seventy-two treatments under the Infant Stimulation program with little change in her condition. Emily recalls the Easter Seals rehab center as having a good program administered by caring people, but she says, "We felt she needed a more intense program."

The Coxes took Colleen back to Yale–New Haven Hospital for further evaluation. It was determined that Colleen's electroencephalogram (EEG) was "consistent with possible ongoing seizure activity and her CT [computer-assisted tomograph] scan with a severe developmental process of the brain." Phenobarbital was prescribed and regularly administered to prevent a possible seizure.

Nonetheless, Colleen did experience a severe seizure and was rushed to the hospital by her frantic parents. The Coxes decided it was necessary to have a medical doctor close by. Her records were transferred to a local neurologist. Emily Cox was discouraged. She says, "All the doctors went just so far with Colleen. Then they sort of threw their hands up in the air and adopted a 'wait and see' attitude. We didn't agree. We felt there had to be help for Colleen somewhere."

On December 13, 1983, Emily took Colleen to Joseph M. O'Reilly, Jr., Ph.D., who at the time was affiliated with the Wholistic Health Center in Brookfield, Connecticut. Emily explains, "We had been going to the Health Center for about four years ourselves and already believed in a nutritional program."

Dr. O'Reilly put Colleen through a battery of tests. Her metabolic function ranged from poor to severely weak. She was deficient in several essential minerals, showed a toxic buildup of some harmful metals. An excess of toxins and low levels of essential minerals, added to the inefficient assimilation of necessary nutrients due to faulty metabolism, are known to cause a multiplicity of problems, including hair loss, weight loss, lack of muscle tone, nervous irritability, weakness, disorientation, colic, constipation, and chronic pain in the joints. Colleen exhibited many classic symptoms.

As a doctor of clinical organic nutrition, Dr. O'Reilly recommended beehive products to correct Colleen's body chemistry and metabolic imbalance, cleanse her blood, improve her circulation, increase the oxygen-carrying capacity of her blood to the brain and glands, and improve the efficiency of her assimilative, digestive, and eliminative functions. In addition, Dr. O'Reilly told Emily to eliminate all foods containing chemical additives, preservatives, flavorings, and colorings from her daughter's diet and insisted Colleen drink only pure spring water, no tap water.

Colleen suffered a "healing crisis" on March 18, 1984. That evening, she developed a low-grade temperature and stuffy nose. It seemed like nothing more than a bit of a cold. But by morning, her temperature had reached a frightening 104°F and a steady discharge of mucus came from her left nostril, which was on her weakest side. Emily says, "My first instinct was to call Colleen's medical doctor for an antibiotic, but Dr. O'Reilly explained a fever is the body's way of burning off infection. He suggested we wait three days, watch her closely, and increase her intake of liquids. That's what we did."

Three days later, Emily took Colleen in to Dr. O'Reilly for an evaluation. The healing crisis had passed, and Colleen was continuing to make progress. Her tongue was pink and healthy. The rings around her eyes were fading and almost gone. Her color was good. Her dazed look had disappeared. Her appetite had improved, and she was trying to drink from a cup. Colleen had begun reaching for objects, and her physical activity had increased.

The happiest news of all was that Colleen had lost the rag-doll floppiness that had characterized her condition a few months earlier. She now clung to her mother when held, just as a healthy child might. Although her daughter still had a long way to go, Emily says thankfully that even the neighbors noticed how much brighter and more alert Colleen had become.

Two short months later, Dr. O'Reilly's progress report on Colleen reflected her continuing improvement. He noted that she was smiling more and was making more sounds. Her eyes fixed with interest on colorful objects. She was able to scoot her little body forward while sitting on the couch. She had rolled over for the first time. Although her left hand and arm still were not functioning normally, she reached with her right hand to remove articles from her face and head. Her skin color was much healthier, and she was able to drink from a cup without difficulty. The family was delighted with Colleen's progress.

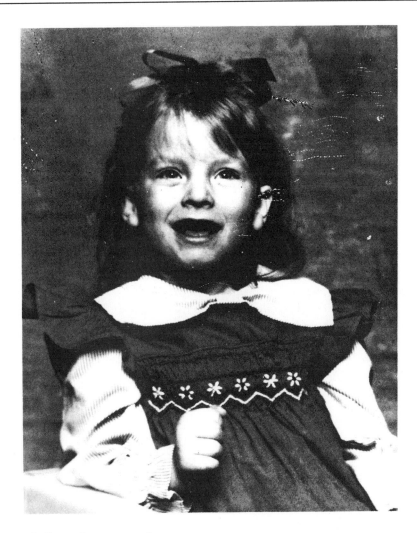

Colleen Cox at age six.

By July 1984, even her physical therapist noticed there was some-thing different about the little girl. She remarked how splendidly Colleen was doing. Dr. O'Reilly's report of that date notes that Colleen's fingernails needed cutting for the first time since she was born. Her hair growth was excellent, and her baby fuzz was completely gone. Her eye contact was good, and she was making meaningful sounds. She showed her displeasure by whining, an important breakthrough. She had begun using her left hand and even attempted to play ball with both hands.

In the spring of 1985, Emily Cox herself reported that her two-and-a-half-year-old daughter "seems more alert as each day passes. She waves bye-bye, plays peek-a-boo. She's not going backward or staying the same. Something in her brain is working! She used to have a 'blank' look, but now we know she understands." She added, "Colleen eats the best. We all want to be as healthy as we can be. We have seen what bee products can do. We use Colleen's guidelines now for the whole family."

Emily reports Colleen's physicians and therapists are astounded at her daughter's steady progress. Given her early diagnosis, Colleen's improvement is something the experts call medically impossible. And Emily says Colleen is continuing to improve.

At ten years of age, Colleen is a sweetly smiling and laughing child. She loves hugs and kisses, and she trustingly shares her shining radiance with all who come in contact with her. The Coxes feel the Lord and His angels watch over children like Colleen with a special kind of love. Between that love and a little help from the bees, Colleen now has a bright future.

previous research conducted in their facility had shown an alcohol-propolis solution was effective in the treatment of unidentified gynecological infections and seeping skin infections. Encouraged by these results, they next isolated fifty-six staph strains and examined the effects of the propolis solution against each one. The antibiotics tested against the same strains included penicillin, ampicillin, methicillin, streptomycin, chloramphenicol, oxytetracycline, erythromycin, and sulfathiazole. Propolis made a very good showing. The scientists determined that "all staphylococcus strains whose sensitivity to propolis was certain were highly resistant to the tested antibiotics. Even strains with low sensitivity to propolis exhibited a wide range of sensitivity to antibiotics. The antibacterial effect of propolis, shown by inhibition of the development of standard strains, was satisfactorily determined."

Covering the same subject is a paper from Czechoslovakia authored by L. Vechet and entitled "Effect of Propolis on Some Species of Microorganisms and Molds." Dr. Vechet also used the staphylococcus bacteria as the microorganism for his study. In this work, a propolis-alcohol solution was compared to penicillin in units of sixteen, eight, and four. To test propolis and a fungicide against molds (fungi), a Saccharomyces yeast was used. Once again, propolis proved more effective than the standard treatment. Dr. Vechet's published conclusion, translated from the Czechoslovakian, states, "Against the staphylococcus bacteria, propolis created inhibition zones, but penicillin did not. The antibiotic effects of the propolis solution correspond to the value of 16 units of penicillin.

"Propolis created a greater field of inhibition in the treatment of mold infection and its effects lasted longer than the effects of the fungicide. The antifungal effects of the propolis solution correspond to 25 units of fungicide."

OLD-TIME PROPOLIS REMEDIES

In the past, no household pharmacopeia was complete without a store of propolis, either in lump, tincture, or tea form. Now it's no longer necessary to brave the bees in order to put propolis in your medicine cabinet. This natural antibiotic is readily available. However, the home remedies from yesteryear are just as effective today as they were then. Here's a peek into the past.

Sore throat. For a sore throat, put a lump of propolis in your mouth and let it melt. The juice is bitter, but the results are remarkable. As you swallow the propolis-rich saliva, your entire throat is treated to a disinfecting antibiotic bath. Swelling is reduced, and the infection usually clears up overnight.

Cuts and scrapes. To guard against infection and promote healing, treat minor cuts and scrapes with propolis tea. Propolis tea can also speed the healing of skin irritations, pimples, acne, and nonspecific skin rashes. Prepare an infusion of propolis by pouring boiling water over a crushed lump of propolis.

Allow it to steep. Pour the resulting tea in a sterile jar and keep it on hand. Apply as needed.

Corns. To get rid of a corn, coat the area with a thick layer of softened propolis and cover. In ages past, country people wrapped a clean cloth around the whole foot, but an adhesive bandage works just as well. Apply more propolis at night before going to bed. The hard corn should soften and be easy to remove in just a few days.

Preventive medicine. Propolis tincture is both a good preventive and a substitute for the propolis tea mentioned above. A tincture is an alcohol-based infusion. Crush a lump of propolis and steep it in pure, food-grade alcoholic spirits. Vodka is excellent. The resulting golden brown liquid can be taken by the teaspoonful, on a sugar cube, or on a square of bread. Taken daily, this time-honored European folk remedy constitutes real preventive medicine.

SHOPPING FOR PROPOLIS

Propolis is a valuable natural healer as well as a very important preventive "medicine" that works safely and naturally to strengthen the system. For apitherapeutical purposes, propolis is offered in various forms. You can buy it as waxy natural chunks, just as it comes from the beehive, or as granules, powder, tablets, capsules, extracts, or liquid tinctures, which contain alcohol. Some particularly effective formulas use propolis in combination with other hive products as well as choice herbs incorporated for their particular properties.

Propolis is the strongest antibiotic found in Nature. It has no toxic side effects, no contraindications, and no upper limits of ingestion. Unlike chemical antibiotics produced in drug laboratories, propolis does not cause the body to build up a tolerance. Ingestors will receive as much benefit from bee propolis utilized during their golden years as from the first bits they ever take. In regular use, propolis builds resistance to respiratory distress, flu, coughs and colds, and more. Propolis assists the immune system and does not inhibit immune action as do lab-produced antibiotics.

When freshly gathered from the hive, propolis is soft and sticky in warm weather, hard and brittle in cold weather. This gold-brown-green substance is a heterogenous mass. It often includes hive debris, plus 20 to 25 percent beeswax. In order to end up with a propolis preparation as rich as possible in the biologically active elements that give propolis its proven powers, it's necessary to start with a chunk of propolis as pure as possible.

The bees themselves select propolis from plants in their flying range that show the highest possible biological resistance. That secretion we see oozing from trees and leaf buds is essential to the defense of the plant. It has measurable biological activity that controls numerous phytopathogenic microorganisms, fungi, and viruses. These defensive secretions are particularly effective in holding back the development of competitive flora, which could steal nutrients and growing space from the trees.

In spite of its scientifically documented valuable properties, propolis is still a stepchild as far as American beekeepers are concerned. Overseas, especially in Russia and surrounding countries, propolis is sought after. It plays an important role in apitherapy clinics, those European health-care establishments that treat various conditions with the products of the beehive. Here at home, there are many beekeeping operations that harvest only honey, just as there are a growing number of large bee yards where both honey and bee pollen are the moneymakers.

But there are just a few commercial harvesters of propolis in the United States. The best propolis comes from the northern climes, where poplar and conifer trees flourish. These trees and their leaf buds produce the highest quality propolis. To those in the know, this is the only propolis worth bragging about.

5

ROYAL JELLY

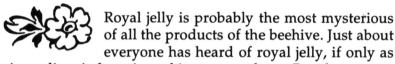 Royal jelly is probably the most mysterious of all the products of the beehive. Just about everyone has heard of royal jelly, if only as an ingredient in luxurious skin-care products. But chances are you don't know much about it as a hormone-rich dietary supplement. Royal jelly is one of Nature's best-kept secrets.

In fact, because royal jelly is fed directly from a worker bee to the queen bee, most beekeepers never have an opportunity to see or taste the royal milk. Nurse bees between five and fifteen days of age secrete royal jelly. In the nursing phase of their development, worker bees practically force-feed themselves near to bursting with an incredibly rich diet of bee pollen and honey. The queen bee drinks her fill of royal jelly directly from the nurse bees' hypopharyngeal glands, located on either side of the nurse bees' heads.

WHAT IS ROYAL JELLY?

Royal jelly is a thick fluid, creamy in consistency, milky white in appearance. It is synthesized in nurse bees' bodies during the digestion of bee pollen, which helps account for its remarkable quantities of hormonal substances and the strong proteins found in its highly nitrogenous composition. It has a pungent odor. The queen bee obviously thinks royal jelly is delicious, but humans find it very tart and bitter on the tongue.

Royal jelly is fed to the queen bee for the whole of her life. This rich royal milk plays an absolutely essential role in the making of a queen. Queen bees are made, not born. Eggs to be reared as queens are laid in specially prepared, super-size brood cells that look rather like peanut shells. But the eggs deposited therein by the queen mother of the hive are identical to those eggs that are destined to become the sexless worker bees of the hive. They are not genetically superior in any way. Worker bees, denied royal jelly except for three short days during the larval period, are the sexless laborers of the hive.

THE COMPOSITION OF ROYAL JELLY

Royal jelly is very complex. A broad chemical analysis reveals that it has a moisture content of 66.05 percent; a protein content of 12.34 percent; lipids, 5.46 percent; reducing substance, 12.49 percent; minerals, .82 percent; and unidentifiable elements, 2.84 percent. And here we are again looking at the "magic" of the bee. As with bee pollen, science still hasn't been able to completely identify and isolate all the important constituents of royal jelly, let alone synthesize a satisfactory substitute in the laboratory.

We know royal jelly is exceptionally rich in natural hormones and offers an abundance of the B vitamins—including thiamine, riboflavin, pyridoxine, niacin, pantothenic acid, biotin, inositol, and folic acid—and vitamins A, C, and E. With twenty amino acids, royal jelly is a highly concentrated source of rich proteins, including cystine, lysine, and arginine. It provides important fatty acids, sugars, sterols, phosphorus compounds, and acetylcholine. Acetylcholine is important in the transmission of nerve messages and assists in the production of glandular secretions. Royal jelly is rich in nucleic acids, which in royal jelly include DNA and RNA, the very stuff of which life is made. Gelatin, one of the precursors of collagen, is another component of royal jelly. Collagen is a powerful anti-aging element that keeps us youthful.

The presence of gamma globulin, an infection-fighting and

immunostimulating factor, has been documented in royal jelly. Not surprisingly, royal jelly also contains decanoic acid, which exhibits strong antibiotic activity against many bacterial and fungal infestations. If royal jelly did not have this built-in antibiotic factor, science points out, the nutritive richness of the royal milk would provide an excellent growing medium for all kinds of harmful microbes. Mother Nature takes care of her own.

Before we examine the scientific studies on royal jelly, let's look at the role this nutritively dense royal milk plays in the hive.

THE REARING OF WORKER BEES

During the first three days of larval development, baby bees destined to become workers of the colony are fed a diluted form of royal jelly—the royal milk liberally mixed with honey. This rich brood food is supplied so generously, the tiny young larvae actually lie in a pool of it within their individual brood cells. The mass feeding of royal jelly comes abruptly to an end after three days. The quality of brood food changes, and the quantity supplied is reduced sharply.

During the remainder of their larval development, baby worker bees are fed bee bread (bee pollen) and honey. Food is given as needed. During the final stages of larval life, the development of the worker-larva's sex glands is suppressed. Her sex glands will remain immature and useless for the whole of her life. However, her hypopharyngeal glands, the glands that will secrete the royal jelly to feed the queen, mature and develop fully. Should royal jelly, even in diluted form, continue to be supplied to these baby workers, a queen would be produced.

THE REARING OF A QUEEN

Throughout her entire larval and pupal periods, a future queen is supplied with highly nutritive, hormone-rich royal jelly. Nurse bees instinctively supply abundant royal jelly to the larvae deposited in the peanut-shaped queen brood cells past the three-day period of mass feeding of royal jelly to all larvae.

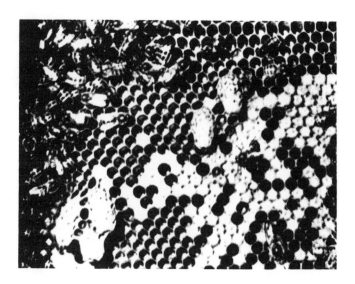

The queen cells on the comb amidst the capped worker brood cells are the peanut-shaped cells.

Without the rich royal milk, a baby queen bee would fail to develop properly. The end result would be merely another worker for the hive. Royal jelly alone is what transforms larvae in queen brood chambers into queens.

As she continues to feed on royal jelly past the three-day cutoff for workers, the queen grows a modified stinger. Unlike those of worker bees, the queen's stinger is curved, not straight. The queen's guard bees take care of hive defense, so the queen herself will never need to sting an intruder or give her life to protect the entrance to the hive. Because the queen uses her stinger only to defend her royal right to rule, she can also retract it after shooting out venom. Unlike a worker bee, the queen does not die after stinging.

There are other major differences in the developmental process, too. As an adult, the queen will have no wax glands. The worker bees build the comb. The queen will have no pollen baskets on her back legs. The workers forage for the foodstuffs of the hive, nectar and pollen, and for propolis. And the queen will have no hypopharyngeal glands to secrete royal jelly. Nurse bees produce royal jelly.

The queen's sex organs progress to fully ripe maturity as she passes through the larval and pupal stages of her development. When she emerges as a royal adult queen, her body is noticeably larger and clearly superior to that of her sisters, the sexless workers of the hive. An average queen bee measures 17 millimeters and weighs 200 milligrams, compared to 12 millimeters and 125 milligrams for worker bees. Royal jelly gives the royal beauty a 42 percent increase in size and a 60 percent superiority in weight over the workers of her court.

Nature builds in yet another advantage. Because the queen is so necessary to the colony, her royal development to full adulthood is accomplished in just sixteen days, thanks to her richly royal diet, compared to the twenty-one days it takes a worker to reach maturity. She has another advantage, too. Her life span is measured in years while a worker bee's life span is measured in weeks. A queen lives forty times longer than the ladies of her court. In the wild, a queen lives productively for five to seven years. Worker bees are worn out and die on an average between the ages of six weeks to eight weeks. Workers are expendable. The queen is not.

During her remarkably extended life span, the queen will lay up to 2,000 eggs per day. Each batch of brood has a total weight greater than two and a half times the queen mother's own body weight.

The queen feasts on royal jelly her entire lifetime. This miraculous food alone is what insures the queen's superior development and incredible longevity. Remember, a queen does not start off with an inborn genetic superiority. The direct feeding of each and every cell of her body with richly nutritive royal jelly is what first creates and then sustains the queen's superiority for the whole of her extra-long life.

To find out what royal-jelly supplementation can do for humans, let's see what science has to say.

THE PROPERTIES OF ROYAL JELLY

Royal jelly has long been credited with miraculous rejuvenating and regenerating properties. Legends tell of Oriental potentates who enjoyed renewed sexual power and lived remarkably long lives with a diet of royal jelly. The basis for the long-held belief that royal jelly possesses some mysterious miraculous element that extends the normal life span is based on the scientific fact of the queen bee's existence.

But what about studies on the royal substance itself? There is continuing research on royal jelly worldwide that has resulted in hard evidence showing royal jelly really can make a substantial contribution to man.

For an overview on the oral ingestion of royal jelly, let's look at a paper entitled "Biology, Biochemistry, and the Therapeutic Effects of Royal Jelly in Human Pathology." This twelve-page paper, written by Dr. A. Saenz and published by the Pasteur Institute of Paris in July 1984, will let you in on the part royal jelly can play in enhancing the quality of life as we get older. You don't have to wade through twelve pages, however. I have lifted out pertinent excerpts. The following is Dr. Saenz's encouraging opening statement: "Each day we add to the therapeutic arsenal of substances that can slow aging and extend the length of the life cycle. In this regard, royal jelly continues to interest the scientist, the biologist, and the physician. Numerous analyses of royal jelly show that 3 percent of its constituents remain an undetermined fraction. The presence of these unidentifiable elements could explain the remarkable and mysterious properties of royal jelly."

Here's yet another product of the beehive with a touch of the bees' magic in it. I suppose some day science will figure out what these unidentifiable elements are and some researcher will try to manufacture them. Until then, the only place to get these mystery nutrients is from the bees.

Of all the vitamins and other nutrients in royal jelly, Dr. Saenz singles out pantothenic acid for special mention. He calls it the longevity factor. Royal jelly contains an abundance of pantothenic acid. This B vitamin is not only necessary for the efficient processing of nutrients in the human body, it also helps arm the body against infection. More importantly, studies with lab animals show a significant increase in the average life span of white mice when a sufficient amount of pantothenic acid is added to their food.

Arteriosclerosis, which used to be called hardening of the arteries, is a condition long associated with the normal aging process. As we get older, our arteries can become inelastic and hard. Today, we know cholesterol is the culprit. Arteries become narrowed due to the buildup of cholesterol on blood-vessel walls, interfering with the free flow of blood. Are you monitoring your diet to keep your cholesterol levels down? Perhaps royal jelly can help.

Dr. Saenz says, "The action of royal jelly in arteriosclerosis is extremely interesting. Blood electrophoresis of atherosclerotic victims shows an abnormal reading. When those who are suffering from high blood-serum cholesterol take royal jelly, the readings correct themselves."

Because I don't have access to the original research, just the published statements of Dr. Saenz, I almost hesitate to give you these next bits of information concerning conditions notoriously difficult to treat. Because Dr. Saenz wrote his paper for his fellow doctors, who are familiar with the studies he refers to, these statements are brief. Nonetheless, the information may be helpful to some of you. So, in Dr. Saenz's words:

> Royal jelly offers significant improvement in another arterial disorder, Buerger's disease (thromboangetis obliterans). . . .
>
> Binet demonstrated royal jelly's effectiveness with the mental disturbances of the aged and in cases of senility in general. . . .
>
> Dr. Livaditis of Greece has published several studies of patients suffering from arthritis who were helped by royal jelly. . . .
>
> A satisfactory remission of Parkinson's disease has been obtained by royal jelly, including a marked reduction of the trembling caused by this affliction. These early clinical trials suggest further study is indicated to understand the beneficial action royal jelly offers victims of neurological disorders.

Dr. Saenz also remarks on the use of royal jelly in what he

calls deficiency states, referring to malnutrition, slow convalescence after illness or an operation, physical or mental exhaustion, loss of appetite, and abnormal loss of weight caused by
anorexia nervosa. He cites the case of an anorexic sixteen-year-
old girl who was considered incurable. This young woman was
hospitalized and kept alive with transfusions of blood and
hydrolyzed proteins. However, when she was given royal jelly,
she gained almost ten pounds in one month, finally regained
her appetite, and began eating normally again.

In the conclusion to his paper, Dr. Saenz says, "We are not
yet fully acquainted with all the mysteries of royal jelly. The
beneficial action of royal jelly is due to the presence of various
substances harmoniously bound to one another and mutually
reinforcing their effects. Royal jelly allows man to recover his
biological balance and confront aging with optimism and se-
renity. In the extremely complex biological product that is royal
jelly, Nature has created a genuine panacea for the aged, or, to
put it simply, for the adult who wishes to extend the limits of
the natural aging process."

Researchers in Argentina have been working with royal jelly
for a considerable length of time. The following paper,
authored by J. R. Lamberti and L. G. Cornejo and translated
from the Spanish, is entitled "Presence of Gamma Globulin in
Injectable Royal Jelly and Its Use in Revitalizing Processes."
The work by Lamberti and Cornejo cited here shows the protective effects of royal jelly. These effects were confirmed by
Dr. L. L. Mandrile of the National University of La Plata.

Even more exciting, Lamberti and Cornejo have documented
important elements in royal jelly that can help slow the aging
process. It just may be that we are close to discovering a factual
basis for all those stories of rejuvenation and longevity. Here's
what the scientists say about gamma globulin: "Gamma globulin is of incalculable value to the living body. Gamma globulin
is the most important component of the proteins that work
internally in the fight against bacteria, viruses, and toxins."

Before the experiments were begun, the patients' blood was
analyzed for gamma globulin levels. After the patients began
receiving their daily injections of the royal-jelly solution, they

Born—1899
Reborn—1979

In 1964, retired at age sixty-five, Noel Johnson was refused life insurance because of a weak and damaged heart. His doctor prohibited physical activity, cautioned him to not even mow the lawn, saying, "You might not live to trim the borders."

At age eighty, Johnson wrote A Dud at 70—A Stud at 80—And How to Do It. *In this book, Johnson tells how he discovered what he calls his second lifetime, a return to full, vigorous manhood and vital health. He explains how he conquered impotence. He says, "I learned bee products have more sex hormones than any other foods. I don't think there has ever been one senile old man in this world who was sexually potent. If you can be sexually active, you'll never grow old. Old age and impotence go hand-in-hand. Bee products provide me with all necessary nutrients, plus the vital hormones which stimulate and nourish the sex glands of both men and women."*

In 1989, at age ninety, Johnson wrote The Living Proof—I Have Found the Fountain of Youth. *In it, he describes his health regimen, a four-part program called the Secrets of Regeneration, which he also discussed in his first book. The Fountain of Youth regimen is what transformed Noel from the sick and impotent old man he was in the late 1970s into the dynamic individual he is today. It encompasses exercise, breathing techniques, mind power, and the dynamite nutrition of bee products. Johnson says, "I have made the products of the beehive the solid foundation of my nutritional program. Although I eat a large variety of whole foods, bee products are an unvarying part of my diet."*

The exercise part of Johnson's regime includes both boxing and running. He's a born competitor. Although he never made a career of it, Noel was a talented amateur boxer in his youth. It was the old-time "fighter" in him that prompted him to jump into action when he was seventy years old. In Noel's own words, "I stripped down and looked in the mirror. All the classic signs of aging were there. I was 40 pounds overweight, with a bulging gut, dull eyes, slack unused muscles. I

Dinner with the king was Noel's reward for completing a Thai marathon in 1987.

looked defeated. But I used to be a fighter. The thought 'defeated' stirred something in my ego. I knew I was doing everything wrong, so I decided to teach myself to live right."

Talk about success stories! Noel, indeed, learned how to stay healthy. Today, he holds the title of World's Senior Boxing Champion, often fighting much younger men to a standstill to keep it. His running schedule is grueling. Beginning with his first marathon in 1977, he usually brings home the gold medal in the Senior Division.

Just crossing the finish line at the twenty-six-plus-mile mark is an accomplishment many marvel over. Johnson runs the world. He has competed in marathons in London, Hawaii, Australia, Japan, and Scandinavia. In Bangkok, Thailand, he even ran a "command performance" that included dinner with the king!

What's his secret? Bee products, Noel says. "I discovered the bee's gifts at age 70. These perfect live foods have restored my manhood, brought me to full vigor and sexual potency, and continue to nourish every cell in my body. I am improving in every way. I don't spend five cents on medicine. I know what you have to do to keep your cells alive and strong. I was not proud of myself at 70. Now, I'm proud of what I can do on the dance floor, in the ring, on the track, and in bed. I am physically able to do whatever I want to do—ballroom dancing, square dancing, long-distance and marathon running, plus championship boxing. You name it and I'll do it—and have—all since I passed 70 years of age."

Noel on the dance floor.

had their blood analyzed anew on a regular basis to establish the effects of the substance. According to the report on those effects, "Subsequent analysis revealed a marked revitalization and visible increase in the activity of the protective mechanisms of the body."

Any substance that has a measurable effect on the immune system is important. But that's not all that was discovered in Argentina. Do you know what collagen is? This fibrous protein component forms connective tissue, including the fibers of the tendons, ligaments, cartilage, and bone. As we age, we slowly lose the ability to renew collagen. Although royal jelly itself doesn't contain collagen, it does contain the building blocks of collagen.

"Royal jelly also contains a gelatinous amino acid, which is a basic component of collagen," say Lamberti and Cornejo in their report. "The deterioration of collagen is obvious in and specific to the aging process. Once it was said human beings had the age of their arteries, but at the present time, one can say more precisely that human beings have the age of their collagen. The aging organism should maintain and remake its collagen, an element of first importance for the body."

At the close of the experiments, the Argentine researchers were more than satisfied with the results they obtained. It's no wonder some of their enthusiasm comes through in their concluding statements:

> In addition to polyvitamins, pluriminerals, and pluriamino acids, royal jelly also includes elements of particular importance for the treatment of aging. During the aging process, the functions of the body diminish progressively. It is necessary to apply early treatment for slowing these decaying organic stages.
>
> We have to resort immediately to elements having a visible revitalizing action. The most important of these is royal jelly, a substance that reduces the destructive effects of time. At present, we can state that royal jelly makes a matchless contribution in this direction and is a first-rate therapeutic. Its gamma globulin and gelatinous collagen

content are of high value, particularly when injected because direct assimilation assists blood-chemical composition dramatically.

The results we obtained with injectable royal jelly administered to the human body were promising and encouraging. With the documentation of gamma globulin and the precursor of collagen among the components of royal jelly, these results become of paramount importance for medicine. Royal jelly is a medicine that justifies thorough studies toward offering mankind a complete therapeutic, particularly for the aged, who are too often neglected.

From the University of Sarajevo comes a paper, translated from the Slavic, entitled "Clinical Value of Royal Jelly and Propolis Against Viral Infections." Many studies exist showing the documented antiviral effects of propolis. The authors of this paper, B. Filipic and M. Likvar, wanted to find out if combining propolis with royal jelly would increase the antiviral properties. It did.

All over the world, scientists are trying to manufacture effective antiviral drugs that will work against selected viruses. So far, success has eluded them. Antiviral substances can be divided into two groups: chemically synthesized compounds and natural compounds. Opinions about the value of these two types of compounds differ, but natural antiviral substances are more valuable because they are not toxic to living cells. Even if they don't work, they can't hurt.

Hive products, including royal jelly and propolis, have a clinically pronounced effect. In orthodox medicine, the best known antiviral substance is interferon. Studies show interferon is effective against herpes viruses, influenza viruses, varicella zoster virus (VSV), and vaccinia virus (cowpox). Interferon is produced by the body in response to a viral infection, but it can also be synthesized in a laboratory.

The problem with manmade interferon is that it can cause side effects, including fever, headache, sore muscles, fatigue, nausea, vomiting, hair loss, and abnormal bleeding. Manufactured interferon is still in the trial phase. Currently, it is approved for use only in the treatment of hairy cell leukemia, but researchers are testing it against other life-threatening viral infections, including AIDS (acquired immune deficiency syndrome).

A total of 220 persons was involved in this study. Of these subjects, about half were given a placebo. In the remaining number, some were treated with royal-jelly-and-propolis combinations of varying strengths, some with royal-jelly-and-interferon combinations. The researchers found:

> In high concentration, royal jelly and propolis alone both have antiviral effects. A proper combination of royal jelly, propolis, and honey had a very obvious antiviral effect, especially against influenza, even diluted one to ten. The combination with 2 percent royal jelly was very effective against vaccinia virus. Against vesicular stomatitis virus, the most effective mixtures included 10 percent royal jelly (without interferon) and 2 percent royal jelly (with interferon added).
>
> Among those persons treated with royal jelly–propolis compounds, only 6 percent suffered viral infections. In the unprotected control group, close to 40 percent became ill.

If you have been paying attention, it probably won't come as a surprise that royal jelly, like bee pollen and propolis, exhibits strong cancer-fighting properties, as witnessed by the following article. The study discussed was a joint effort of three prestigious Canadian facilities: the Ontario Agricultural College in Guelph, the Department of National Health and Welfare in Ottawa, and the University of Toronto. The article, which was published in *Nature* in May 1959, is entitled "Activity of 10-Hydroxydecenoic Acid From Royal Jelly Against Experimental Leukemia and Ascitic Tumors."

The research was part of a long-term Canadian study on the chemistry and biological activity of royal jelly. In this particular experiment, the scientists mixed royal jelly with active tumor cells taken from cancerous mice. They report that an injection of the mixture suppressed mouse leukemia and inhibited the formation of tumors. These no-nonsense Canadians didn't fool around either. Here's how they evaluated the results:

> The criterion we used in these experiments was survival. The mice either developed leukemia or tumors or were fully protected. Control mice died from ascitic tumors in less than 14 days, while mice receiving appropriate mixtures of cells and royal jelly all failed to develop tumors. Protected mice were kept under observation for 90 days after death of the control mice. They were then sacrificed and autopsied to confirm the absence of tumors.
>
> These results have been confirmed repeatedly on nearly 1,000 mice during a two-year period and show a striking effect: Either all the mice die quickly, or all survive. Two groups of mice which received tumor cells plus royal jelly remained alive and healthy more than 12 months after inoculation, while sister mice which received the same number of tumor cells without royal jelly died within twelve days.

In other words, the Canadian scientists came up with a vaccine that protects mice against leukemia and the subsequent development of related tumors. That's not too exciting, is it? However, remember that work with lab animals always precedes experimental trials of a promising vaccine on human volunteers. Our children and grandchildren may be as routinely inoculated against cancer as the youngsters of today are against mumps and measles. What a grand and glorious possibility!

In conclusion, we turn to an article by the German physician Hans Weitgasser. Dr. Weitgasser's article is entitled "Royal Jelly in Dermatological Cosmetics" and includes material subtitled "Experiences With Royal Jelly in the Medicinal-Cosmetic Practice." It ran in the German publication *Medizinische Kosmetick.*

You are probably familiar with royal jelly as an ingredient in luxurious and costly skin-care products. Perhaps you think the cost of such products outweighs their benefits. Or perhaps you think the claims made for such products are so extraordinary that they can't possibly be true. Dr. Weitgasser disagrees. He says, "Through local application, as an ingredient in face masks, creams, and lotion, royal jelly has tremendous effects at the cellular level. In regular use, the skin becomes soft and wrinkles disappear. When royal jelly is used topically as a salve on skin damaged by the effects of radium treatment, the skin heals rapidly and symptoms disappear." In other words, Dr. Weitgasser concludes, everything you've heard of royal jelly's benefits to the skin is factual.

THE EUPHORIC EFFECTS OF ROYAL JELLY

The term "euphoria" comes from the Greek and signifies "a state of well-being." In the jargon of the psychologist, "euphoria" has come to mean an "exaggerated feeling of well-being, one that has no basis in truth or reality."

In the case of royal jelly, the euphoric effect has been well established. It is very real. However, physicians call royal jelly's effect a false euphoria. Medical experts warn against the feelings this incredibly powerful and potent substance from the beehive provides. This is because the natural "high" royal jelly brings travels through the body like a jolt of electricity. Even someone taking royal jelly for the first time will usually feel a dynamic surge of energy and well-being pulsing through his entire body.

The entire organism responds dramatically to the influx of the concentrated nutrients present in royal jelly. Energy levels peak and a feeling of invincibility pervades the body. Even those who are ill seem suddenly to feel almost miraculously better. And therein lies the danger. It is important to understand that the euphoric effects of royal jelly are sometimes so strong, they can actually mask symptoms that require the attention of a doctor.

On the other hand, the scientifically documented benefits of royal jelly are many and varied, as already discussed. And who can deny it's wonderful to feel full-to-bursting with youthful energy and well-being? Just be sure the wonderful feeling of euphoria royal jelly brings doesn't stop you from seeking medical treatment should you have a condition that calls for a visit to your physician.

A SCIENTIFIC SUMMING UP

To wind up the scientific portion of this chapter, I want to share with you the closing statement of a lecture given before the German Medical Association in October 1956. Dr. H. W. Schmidt's lecture was entitled "Royal Jelly in Diet, Prophylaxis, and Therapy."

"The effects of the active substances and nutrients contained in royal jelly take place throughout the entire body," Dr. Schmidt said. "This bitter-tasting royal milk from the bees helps normalize and regulate all the functions of the human body. From all the investigations and observations that have been made with royal jelly, it is apparent that this substance is a powerful agent composed of hormones, nutrients, enzymes, and biocatalysts. Royal jelly revives and stimulates the functions of cells and the secretion of glands. It also steps up the metabolism, and stimulates the circulatory system.

"To summarize," Dr. Schmidt said, "authoritative sources now believe it is the interplay of all the complex factors present in royal jelly that works to preserve life and strength in the organism, that delays the aging process and helps the organism retain for as long as possible the physical freshness of the body, elasticity of the mind, and psychic buoyancy of youth."

Clearly, royal jelly not only leaves users feeling full-to-bursting with youthful energy but also with praise.

SHOPPING FOR ROYAL JELLY

For many years, I personally ate my way through a pound of liquid royal jelly every two months, at the rate of one teaspoonful of this acidic, bitter-tasting royal milk per day. I never did grow to like it, but because of its potent properties, I took it anyway. During this period, my company handled only liquid royal jelly. Knowing my vow to have only the best bee product of its kind, you will understand I believed back then this was the best royal jelly obtainable.

In 1981, I discovered I was wrong. Betty Lee Morales, a personal friend and perhaps the greatest female health authority on natural health care who ever lived, was the one who straightened me out. Betty Lee introduced royal jelly to the Hollywood stars right after World War II. As the word got out, everyone wanted royal jelly. Betty Lee's success with royal jelly was based on careful formulation and strong scientific documentation, but some unscrupulous manufacturers also jumped on the bandwagon. The claims for royal jelly got so wildly improbable that the Food and Drug Administration (FDA) stopped the importation of all royal jelly, including Betty Lee's.

Nonetheless, Betty Lee's research was solid. Betty Lee convinced me that the liquid royal jelly I was eating with such confidence was not the royal jelly served to the queen bee. She explained that it is impossible to get *liquid* royal jelly fresh enough to have all the potent properties intact. In liquid form, royal jelly begins to deteriorate immediately after harvest. The royal jelly the queen feasts on is never more than twenty-four hours old. When Betty Lee Morales tested the biological activity of twenty-four-hour royal jelly and compared its activity to that of royal jelly that was forty-eight hours old, she documented her results. What Betty Lee's tests confirmed is that twenty-four-hour royal jelly is close to *four times* more biologically active than royal jelly just forty-eight hours old.

The conclusions were obvious. Twenty-four-hour royal jelly is what gives the queen bee her extraordinary powers. Freshly secreted royal jelly transforms an ordinary bee larva into the superior queen. Fresh royal jelly sipped from the hypopharyngeal glands of the nurse bees activates the queen's sex glands, helps her lay up to 2,000 eggs per day with a total weight greater than that of her own body, and extends her life span so dramatically. The queen lives forty times longer than the sexless worker bees, denied royal jelly.

Betty Lee told me the purveyors of liquid royal jelly don't want you to know when their products were harvested. Due to the time required to harvest, process, package, and ship the vials, most liquid forms of royal jelly are at least thirty to ninety days old. Betty Lee concluded that twenty-four-hour royal jelly is perhaps fifty times more biologically active than royal jelly that is a month old.

From Betty Lee, I learned that the only way to halt the rapid deterioration of royal jelly is to freeze-dry the royal milk on-site directly after harvest. Freeze-drying is simply a super-quick way of removing all the moisture in a substance. What's left behind is a powder that contains every bit of the substance except the water.

Then Betty Lee Morales carried my education a giant step further. The formula Betty Lee favored contains twenty-four-hour royal jelly plus bee pollen and bee propolis. This mating of all three of the active products of the beehive is a natural. She explained that her research showed twenty-four-hour royal jelly is immensely potentiated by the addition of pollen and propolis. She also revealed another fact. In her search for absolute perfection, Betty Lee discovered that natural vitamin E greatly potentiates all three beehive products.

When shopping for royal jelly, check the label carefully. First of all, know your source. Because of the reasons set forth above, I believe the most dynamic royal jelly formula will contain all the products of the beehive plus vitamin E but very little else. Don't shop for royal jelly on price alone. Unless the label tells you the royal jelly in the product is freeze-dried, it's very likely the end product will be weak in potency, possibly totally inactive. Check also to see just how much royal jelly is contained in the product. If royal jelly is far down the ingredient list, with many tableting aids and additives preceding it, you can be sure that not much of this expensive, hard-to-harvest ingredient is in the end product.

6

HONEY

 You probably already know that bees make honey from the nectar they sip from the hearts of flowers. What you may not know is just how hard the bees have to work to produce one spoonful of that sweetly nutritious liquid gold you drizzled on your cereal this morning. Prepare to be amazed.

When a bee alights on a blossom, she sucks up a drop of nectar with her proboscis and puts it in her honey sac. The process of turning nectar into honey begins in the foraging bee's honey sac. To completely fill her honey sac, the bee may fly as many as three miles total, visiting one flower after another, taking a tiny sip of nectar from each one.

Once back in the hive, a receiving bee helps the forager unload, transferring the nectar in turn to her honey sac. The honey-making process continues in the sac of the receiving bee. When this internal enriching and concentrating process is completed, the receiving bee puts drops of the still-fluid nectar in empty cells on the comb. Up to three-quarters of the water content must be removed before the enriched liquid nectar can ripen. To give you an idea of the amount of work the bee still has to do to turn nectar into honey, you should know nectar contains from 40 to 80 percent water. Fully ripened honey contains only 18 to 20 percent water. There's still a lot of work ahead.

To assist in the necessary evaporation process, worker bees

transfer each tiny drop of nectar first from one cell to another, then to another, and then to still another. With each transfer, the nectar loses a micromolecule of moisture to the air. When the enriched nectar thickens sufficiently, it is put into a honeycomb cell. At this point, however, the nectar is still too wet. To further evaporate the excess moisture, many bees band together and fan their wings over the filled combs. With hundreds of sisters beating their wings in unison, a mighty current of air sweeps over the unripe honey nectar, hastening the moisture removal.

When sufficient moisture has evaporated, only then will the bees seal the filled comb with wax. Inside the sealed comb, the honey will continue ripening. Because of the efficient waxen "packaging" provided by the bees, honey in the comb will keep for many years. Many people say honey eaten from the comb has the best flavor of all.

To produce a single pound of honey, the bees must bring in around 75,000 loads of nectar and then process it as described above. For one single pound of honey, the sisters of the hive will fly the equivalent of four to six times the circumference of the Earth. A busy bee colony can produce up to 300 pounds of honey in a single season.

THE COMPOSITION OF HONEY

You may think of honey merely as a golden syrup that tastes delicious on your morning toast, which it is. But this sweet gift from the beehive is a lot more than just delicious. It is highly nutritious.

The composition of honey varies according to the source of the nectar, but all varieties of raw honey are nutrient-rich. I am not talking about strained and clarified commercially processed honey here. For example, studies show commercially processed, clarified, strained honeys lose from 33 to 50 percent of their original vitamin content. It is important to emphasize that raw, unprocessed honey is the type that is valued for its nutrient content and medicinal properties.

Honey contains as many as eighty different substances important in human nutrition. The sugar content of honey is well known. The major sugars in fully ripe honey are glucose and fructose, which are easily assimilated monosaccharides (simple sugars). Monosaccharides pass directly into the blood without being processed by the body. Glucose is so compatible with the human organism, it can be injected directly into the blood. In contrast, the disaccharides in refined white table sugar are foreign. Disaccharides have to be broken down in the small intestine before entering the bloodstream.

Honey contains important vitamins, minerals, and trace elements. In the vitamin category, honey offers vitamin A, beta-carotene, all of the B-complex vitamins, and vitamins C, D, E, and K. Among the mineral salts, it offers magnesium, sulfur, phosphorus, iron, calcium, chlorine, potassium, iodine, sodium, copper, and manganese.

Raw honey also contains live enzymes, important to the internal actions of many systems of the body. The enzyme content of honey is one of the highest of all foods. Honey also contains proteins, carbohydrates, organic acids, hormones, and antimicrobial and antibiotic factors.

And honey contains a small quantity of an unknown substance, another mysterious enrichment courtesy of the bees, an element science cannot identify, cannot synthesize, cannot manufacture.

HONEY THROUGH THE AGES

The Greeks viewed honey as one of Nature's most precious gifts. Ancient Egyptians and Greeks used it extensively. In the oldest medical papyri of Egypt (circa 2600–2200 B.C.), the formula for a standard wound salve calls for "byt" (honey), "mrht" (grease), and "ftt" (lint). In records dating back to 1553–1550 B.C., honey was prescribed to heal wounds, to stimulate urination, and to ease pain in the belly. By actual count, honey was the most-used medicament in ancient Egypt. Of the over 900 different remedies recorded, more than 500 were honey-based.

The ancient Egyptians, Assyrians, Chinese, Greeks, and Romans also prescribed honey. They used it for open wounds as well as problems of the stomach. Hippocrates of Greece prescribed honey for many diseases. Detailing one of his many honey-based remedies, the Father of Medicine wrote, "Honey drink cures phlegm and calms down cough." Hippocrates is known to have prescribed "oxymel" (vinegar and honey) for pain and "hydromel" (water and honey) for thirst and light fevers. For acute fevers, he blended honey, water, and various medicinal herbs.

A contemporary of Hippocrates, Democritus (460–357 B.C.), the Greek philosopher who first postulated the theory that the universe is composed of atoms, was considered an authority on just about everything. When asked how to live long and keep in good health, Democritus answered, "Annoint one's interior with honey, and one's exterior with oil."

Ancient Egyptians and Greeks used honey to preserve meat—and to embalm their dead. The preservative properties of honey are astounding. A royal Egyptian infant, well preserved in a container filled with honey, was discovered in one of the pyramids at Gizeh. When Alexander the Great died in 323 B.C. in the midst of one of his far-flung campaigns, his body was immersed in a vessel of honey and taken back to Macedonia for burial. In the first century A.D., the bodies of honored Jews were embalmed by placing them in honey for long periods.

Among the medicaments inscribed on ancient tablets discovered in Mesopotamia and Assyria, honey is prominently featured. In the Ayurvedic writings of India, tonics to "preserve youth," "prolong life," and "give pleasure" were honey-based.

Galen (A.D. 130–200), the Greek who ultimately made a name for himself as a Roman physician of great renown, called honey the "all-purpose remedy." Galen prescribed honey for intestinal ailments, including gangrenous stomatitis, and for poisoning. You may remember from history class (or from *I. Claudius* on your Public Broadcasting Service channel) that poisoning was a popular method of removing a rival in ancient Rome.

Honey is mentioned favorably in the writings of many religions. It is praised in the Christian Bible and in the holy Koran, the sacred writings of Islam. Concerning the therapeutic value of honey, the following verse appears in the Koran:

Thy Lord has inspired the Bees,
to build their hives in hills,
on trees and in man's habitations.
From within their bodies comes
a drink of varying colors,
wherein is healing for mankind.
Verily, in this is a Sign,
for those who give thought.

In medieval times, Arabian physician Ibn-Sina (A.D. 980–1037), also known as Avicenna, described many honey-based remedies in his *Canon*. He wrote, "Honey helps when you have a runny nose, cheers you up, makes you feel fit, facilitates digestion, gets rid of wind, improves appetite. Honey is a provision for retaining youth, makes the memory better, sharpens the wits." Ibn-Sina wrote of honey's beneficial effect on deep, infected ulcers and used honey to treat open wounds of all kinds. Old Russian manuscripts also detail wound cures accomplished with honey. One says, "Honey takes away the stench from wounds."

Down through history, honey has been an efficient treatment for all open wounds, including war wounds. Honey went to the wars right along with the warriors. From ancient times almost to the present, records show wounds suffered in battle by everyone from the Crusader knights to the soldiers of the Crimean War to the combatants of World War I were treated on the battlefield with wound dressings of honey. Very effective they were, too.

With the advent of modern antibiotics and other manmade drugs, the use of honey as a remedy fell by the wayside. Recently, however, the medical and scientific communities have rediscovered this ancient medicine.

RECENT MEDICAL FINDINGS

Much of the effectiveness of raw honey has been traced to the bee pollen and propolis suspended within it. Because we have already explored much of the scientific data on these products of the beehive in earlier chapters, I'm not going into the properties of raw honey in-depth. However, several studies deserve your attention. Not surprisingly, those ancient battlefield physicians were right.

In "Acceleration of Wound Healing by Topical Application of Honey," an article published in the *American Journal of Surgery* in 1983, Arieh Bergman and colleagues report, "Topical application of raw, unboiled honey was observed to be effective in decubitus ulcers, infected wounds, and burns. Honey is hypertonic and has been shown to be sterile and highly bactericidal.

"In all instances," the Israeli researchers continued, "the area of the wound was smaller and depth of tissue repair was greater in wounds treated with honey. Acceleration of tissue repair was seen when honey was used. Wounds of the honey-treated animals healed much faster than the wounds of the control animals. Our results suggest that honey applied topically on open wounds accelerates the healing process."

From S. Mladenov of Bulgaria comes a report entitled "Diseases of the Air Passages Treated With Honey." I'm not going to ask you to read through all the details involved in treating the 17,862 patients in this study. I'm giving you only brief excerpts of the results. According to the report, honey performed well against a variety of respiratory problems, as follows:

We found honey has bactericidal, anti-allergic, anti-inflammatory, and expectorant properties that insure the body an immunobiological defense and give it the capacity to regenerate its attacked cells. Of 17,862 patients treated with honey, 8,836 were men and 9,026 were women. Most of the patients ranged from 21 to 60 years old. After treatment, the results are:

Chronic bronchitis. Without symptoms—64.41 percent; improved condition—23.5 percent; temporary improvement—6.3 percent; no effect—5.69 percent.

Asthmatic bronchitis. Without symptoms—62 percent; improved condition—26.40 percent; temporary improvement—5.60 percent; no effect—6 percent.

Bronchial asthma. Without symptoms—55.44 percent; long-lasting improvement (fewer and lighter crises)—

30.25 percent; temporary improvement—5.80 percent; no effect—8.51 percent.

Chronic rhinitis. Without symptoms—82 percent; long-lasting improvement—14 percent; no effect—4 percent.

Allergic rhinitis. Without symptoms—62 percent; long-lasting improvement—22 percent; temporary improvement—6 percent; no effect—6 percent.

Sinusitis. Without symptoms—56 percent; long-lasting improvement—14 percent; temporary improvement—16 percent; no effect—14 percent.

According to the conclusion of the report, "The treatment of non-specific diseases of the air passages with honey is efficient when the right honey type and method are used. Treatment with honey is contraindicated for patients with allergy to honey, when in crisis, status asthmaticus, tumors in the air passages, cardiopulmonary insufficiency and fever."

Caution: In medical terminology, "contraindicated" means "not indicated, unsuitable, possibly dangerous." Please take special note of the warnings issued by Mladenov in his conclusion, above. Obviously, it's wrong to give honey to someone who is allergic to it. And, unless the patient is under the care of a physician who recommends it, don't give honey to someone who is seriously ill or has asthma, respiratory tumors, a heart or lung condition, or fever.

This next paper, entitled "The Use of Honey in Natural Therapeutics," was authored by Yves Donadieu of France. It was presented at the Apitherapy Second Symposium hosted by Romania in the mid-1970s. Because Donadieu's concluding statement offers a wide overview, I am using excerpts from it to sum up the use of honey as both food and medicament: "This food was found to be perfectly tolerated, even in very large doses. Honey contains a series of nutritive and power-producing elements. It has an important stimulant action overall. Honey has a light appetite-stimulating effect and facilitates assimilation and digestion of other foods. It also has laxative, sedative, antitoxic, antiseptic, anti-anemic, fever-reducing, and emollient properties."

I suppose we can all agree that honey is a delicious and

nutritious food with health-promoting properties. Is that reason enough for all of us to eat it? Donadieu thinks so. He says, "The healthy man eats honey to counteract the possible shortage of amino acids, minerals, organic acids, and vitamins in certain foodstuffs; for better physical efficiency; for its dynamic and stimulative action on the heart. Honey increases resistance [to disease] and helps strengthen the organism."

Donadieu also says, "The sick man eats honey in the following syndromes: Physical and mental fatigue; during disease or convalescence; aging; abnormal rhythm of the heart; high blood pressure; after serious operations; pharyngitis, laryngitis, rhinitis, sinusitis, general bronchial diseases; coughs of various origins; urine retention; nervous disorders; depression; insomnia, some headaches; infected wounds; ulcerations; burns; pruritis, skin diseases; cramps."

On feeding infants honey, Donadieu believes, "Honey facilitates calcium assimilation and magnesium retention in babies. Babies fed on honey develop better than those fed on sugar."

Caution: In spite of the fact that honey has been routinely fed to babies for hundreds of years, research has recently tied some cases of infant botulism and Sudden Infant Death Syndrome (SIDS) to the feeding of honey to infants. Yes, honey is a nutrient-rich food long thought suitable for babies. However, due to recent findings, feeding honey to infants cannot be recommended.

A 1980 report from the Scientific Board of the California Medical Association entitled "Honey, Infant Botulism and the Sudden Infant Death Syndrome" reinforces this warning. However, it also says, "The safety of honey for older persons with normal intestinal physiology remains unquestioned." The more efficient intestinal tracts of older children and adults are not susceptible to attack by C botulinum bacteria, which are the culprits in infant botulism. In fact, in many ways, honey is indisputably better for the body than sugar.

HONEY VERSUS REFINED SUGAR

Honey is a richly nutritious food as well as a sweetly delicious one. Because refined white table sugar is the sweetener of choice for most Americans, let's compare honey with sugar.

Grandmother's Honey-Based Skin Conditioners

It is said Cleopatra bathed in ass's milk and honey to keep her skin soft and smooth and to enhance her beauty. Well, Cleo had nothing on Gramma. Down through the ages, legendary ladies have used honey-based lotions and potions to nourish and condition their skin. Here are several of Grandmother's prize "receipts," guaranteed to make you glad we now have a drugstore on every corner.

Honey Soap. *I'm not going to ask you to start with lye, ashes, fat, and a big washtub. That was Great-grandmother's way. Here's how Grandmother did it: Cut two pounds of yellow soap into thin slices. Put the soap slices in a heavy pot with enough water to prevent burning. Place the pot on a fire and stir the soap. As soon as all the soap has dissolved, add one pound of honey. Stir until the mixture begins to bubble and boil. Remove the pot from the fire. Add a few drops of rose oil to the mixture and pour the mixture into a deep, flat dish to cool. Cut the hardened soap into squares. Honey soap improves with age.*

Honey Mask. *Mix one tablespoon honey with one tablespoon fine white flour. Add a few drops of rose water, enough to make a smooth paste that's easy to spread. Cleanse your face thoroughly. Apply the honey mask generously over your entire face except around your eyes. Let the pack remain on your face for half an hour, then remove it with tepid water and a soft cloth. This mask will leave your skin soft and velvety.*

Honey Hand Cream. *Rub together one pound of honey with the yolks of eight eggs. Gradually add one pound of sweet almond oil. Work in a half pound of bitter almonds, powdered. Perfume the mixture with two drams each of Attar of Bergamot and Attar of Cloves. This cream makes a very fine softener for the hands.*

Balm of Gilead and Honey Salve. *Put one pint of Balm of Gilead buds in a kettle with one pint of lard (rendered pork fat). Boil slowly for half an hour, stirring often. Strain out the exhausted buds. Add four ounces of mutton tallow, three ounces of honey, three ounces of beeswax, one ounce of castile soap, one ounce of rosin, and one ounce of alum. Cook slowly until done, usually from a half to one hour, stirring often. This salve is excellent for chapped hands and lips, sores and cuts, frostbite, and piles.*

Honey is a natural, nutritious sweet. Sugar is a non-nutrient; it offers only empty calories. Honey is gently metabolized by your body. The energy it provides is easily and naturally used. Refined sugar packs a wallop. It rushes into your bloodstream, jolting your pancreas into action. As your body tries to stabilize your blood sugar, a flood of insulin is pumped out. When the excess sugar is effectively neutralized, your blood-sugar level drops—fast. A sugar rush picks you up, but the letdown is hard and abrupt.

When you compare honey with other common sweeteners, you might decide you get more sweetness for fewer calories with the others. When you compare honey against the others pricewise, you might decide honey is too costly. However, there are variables that should enter into your thinking. For example, to equal the sweetness of one tablespoon of honey, you must use from one and a half to two tablespoons of the other common sweeteners. Then, too, sweet syrups (corn syrup, maple syrup, and molasses) contain approximately 30 percent water, while honey is only around 17 percent water. Honey is actually the better buy.

COOKING WITH HONEY

If you have heard honey will keep baked goods moist and delicious for a long time, that's not an old wives' tale. It's true. Studies show moisture retention in a recipe increases proportionally with the amount of honey substituted for the called-for sugar.

For example, 25 percent honey and 75 percent sugar resulted in a moisture content of 24.8 percent when first baked. At the end of a month, the moisture content dropped to 14.0 percent. Substituting honey for sugar half-and-half (50 percent honey and 50 percent sugar) resulted in a moisture content of 26.6 percent when fresh baked and 18.1 percent after one month.

Because honey contains moisture, the liquid in recipes must be reduced when honey is substituted for dry sugar. These tests showed honey can be used as a sweetening ingredient in baking by up to 50 percent by reducing the liquid called for in the recipe. Honey can be substituted fully for sugar by reducing the liquid *and* by adding baking soda to neutralize the natural acidity of honey.

If you want to substitute nutritious honey for empty-calorie sugar in your recipes, here's the rule: For each one cup of sugar called for in the recipe, substitute one cup of honey plus one-fourth to one-half teaspoon baking soda. Reduce the liquids in the recipe by one-fourth cup total.

To measure honey, use a greased measuring cup. First measure the fat or oil your recipe requires, then measure the honey in the same cup. The fat will form a light coating on the inside of the cup. Even the last drop of honey will slide right out.

To bake with honey, reduce the temperature called for in your recipe by twenty-five degrees to prevent overbrowning. Unless your baking pan is heavy (cast iron, for example), slide a cookie sheet under it. Your honey cakes or cookies will then bake more evenly with less risk of burning on the bottom.

Liquifying honey is not difficult. If you don't use honey often, you may occasionally discover your honey has thickened or developed granulated sugar crystals on the sides and bottom of the jar. To reliquify thick or crystalized honey, simply immerse the jar in a hot-water bath. The honey will revert to a smooth, free-flowing syrup, and the sugar crystals will obligingly dissolve.

SHOPPING FOR HONEY

Because I keep two active beehives behind my garage, I often slice out a piece of warm comb dripping with honey. I promise you, this is one of Mother Nature's sweetest treats. However, in my family, we use a lot of honey, more than my bees produce. Therefore, I also buy raw honey in gallon jars from a local beekeeper.

If you aren't acquainted with a friendly beekeeper, shop for raw, unprocessed honey. Your health-food store is an obvious source, but most supermarkets carry at least some raw honey. Read the labels.

7

Bee Products for Animals

 By now, you've read about all those studies in which animals ranging from the usual laboratory mice to sheep to hens to rabbits, even cows, were used to research the effects of bee products. Those closely monitored clinical animal studies have well and truly—medically and scientifically—documented the many benefits that follow when the diet is supplemented with bee products. So, it surely won't come as a surprise to discover that hive products are just as right for domesticated animals as they are for people and lab animals.

I've learned quite a bit about the special needs of horses since the equine division of my company came into being, but I don't profess to be an expert in that field. Accordingly, I've asked Buzz Kennedy to help me out with this chapter. Buzz is the founder and president of the equine division of my company.

BEE BENEFITS FOR HORSES

Bee pollen is a complete food, "manufactured" by Mother Nature. It contains no drugs, legal or illegal. There are some very real benefits connected with supplying bee products to horses, as well as to all living things. Remember, all effects are backed up by hard scientific data.

Here's a sample of what trainers and breeders who feed their stock bee pollen can expect:

- *Recovery.* In a two-year double-blind study, it was shown that subjects eating bee pollen recovered quickly after stressed performances, requiring less time to re-establish normal body rhythms (blood pressure and breathing) than the controls. Even more dramatic, some subjects actually bettered their time on a second go around the track immediately after completing a hard run.

- *Swelling.* Clinical tests showed that the swelling of limbs and joints common after a hard race can be markedly relieved by the regular feeding of bee pollen. Up to a half-inch reduction in swelling just twenty minutes after going the distance has been documented.

- *Red blood.* Maybe your stock is all "blue bloods," but blue bloods run on red blood just the same. Studies have shown bee pollen can increase the red-blood-cell (hemoglobin) count by up to 30 percent.

- *Oxygenation.* As the production of hemoglobin is stepped up, richly oxygenated blood courses swiftly through the body, resulting in a measurable increase in strength, stamina, speed, and endurance. This important advantage enables an animal to stay the course and finish tougher.

- *Bleeding.* Studies have shown 80 to 90 percent of all horses that put forth maximum effort are bleeders. Bee products strengthen arteries, veins, and capillaries to offer maximum protection against bursting and can assist in healing minor damage that has already occurred.

- *Fertility.* Not surprisingly, bee products can help strengthen the reproductive system of both mares and stallions. Research from the University of California estimates a mare will foal on average only five times in ten years. Breeders have found bee products help improve the odds.

- *Worming.* When a horse is wormed with chemical drugs, *all* intestinal bacteria are destroyed, including the necessary

This Old Gray Mare Is *Better* Than She Used to Be

In 1986, the equine division of my company was born. You already know that my company grew out of my personal search for the best bee pollen in the world. Here's where you find out how Buzz Kennedy's fondness for an old gray mare led to the development of an entire division for horses. An old-time horseman, Buzz is the founder and president of the equine division. Buzz tells what happened:

"When I was in the market for a stable pony, I ended up coming home with a little gray filly. I guess you could say she chose me. She stretched her neck over the door of her stall as I walked past and nipped me on the behind. I clutched the spot, hollered 'Ouch!' and turned around to see the gray laughing at me. I swear that little gal had a twinkle in her eye. She shook her head, whuffed at me, and got her nicely combed, 'please buy me' mane in a tangle. I needed a stable stable pony, a workhorse, not a prima donna. I glared at her and walked on. I looked over the rest of the stock but kept coming back to that little gray filly. I ended up forking over $700 and took her home to the ranch.

"Because she was such a good nanny, we called her Mary Poppins. When she worked, she tended to business and worked hard. My pedigreed bloods got a real workout keeping up with that high-stepping little gal. When Poppy, for short, was off duty, she still frisked around like a colt, even as she got older. She pranced like the thoroughbred she wasn't when she took one of the high-bred bloods out to the paddock. With her friendly nature, Poppy became a favorite. Like a mischievous child, Poppy exasperated me sometimes, but I've never been sorry I bought her.

"As the years went by, Poppy got tired. She'd come back from the first run of the morning blowing and short of breath. She would jerk her head up and down, and her sides would heave as she tried to get enough air. We gave her longer and longer breaks between workouts. Eventually, Poppy couldn't give the bloods enough exercise anymore. Then Poppy lost interest in eating. Even oats didn't tempt her. I tried

Mary Poppins (Poppy)

a little extra molasses, special vitamins, even liquid food supplements. But those old standbys didn't work. She was off her feed for sure. I tell you, folks, I felt bad. Poppy had been a good and faithful employee for five years. More than that, she was a friend. Reluctantly, I began thinking about replacing her.

"Then I remembered reading about the spectacular results super-trainer Charles Whittingham had been racking up ever since he started feeding his horses bee pollen back in 1981. I knew that Royden Brown's company was located in my home state of Arizona. When I was looking over the stock at the horse show in Scottsdale [Arizona] Horse Park in February 1986, I gave those friendly folks a call and ended up getting some bee pollen for Poppy. She didn't seem to like it at first but did nibble a few grains from the palm of my hand. I guess the fresh, sweet taste won her over. Soon she was watching for me and nuzzling around, sniffing my pockets looking for her morning bee-pollen treat.

"Then I started sprinkling bee pollen on her mash, and her appetite came back full force. It wasn't long before she was chomping hay again and prancing out in the morning eager for a hard run. Instead of needing a break between exercise sessions, she snorted just like she used to and signaled her readiness to go again. Her coat lost its dullness and became glossy and thick. Even her attitude improved. She got that old mischief back in her eyes.

"When I saw what those golden granules had done for Poppy, you better believe I became a believer. Whittingham was on to something. We started giving all the stock a ration of bee pollen. That's when we saw some very interesting side effects. Even after a hard workout, the horses were puffing and blowing less. Not only Poppy; the thoroughbreds also seemed ready to go again immediately. That was terrific, but we had another surprise.

"All the horses seemed to be traveling better when we hauled them from track to track around the country. Even the bloods, with their delicate digestive systems, adjusted quickly to the differences in hay and water wherever we went. We no longer had to factor time lags for adjustment periods into our schedules when we went on the road.

"I decided to look into this phenomenon. To say I was impressed with the mountains of scientific data on the 'world's only perfect food' is an understatement. I was even more impressed with Poppy's near-miraculous turnaround and extremely pleased with the increase in stamina and endurance our thoroughbreds showed after we added bee pollen to their feed.

"It was in 1986 that I joined Royden Brown's company. I'm proud to tell you that the equine division I head up is putting out some mighty powerful bee-pollen products especially for horses. My mama taught me to share the good things in life. Bee products certainly qualify.

"And, yes, Poppy's still going strong."

friendly bacteria. Without the digestive bacteria needed to process nutrients, a horse gradually loses energy and vigor. Specially formulated bee products can prevent the need for chemical deworming several times per year.

- *Wood chewing.* Even stables that feed good-quality alfalfa hay and appropriate vitamin and mineral supplements can have seemingly healthy horses who "eat" their corrals. Wood chewing—gnawing on the sides of a stall—is a sure sign something's missing from a horse's feed. From all reports, supplementing a wood chewer's diet with bee products will end the problem.

- *Coat improvement.* One effect on which all trainers and breeders who feed their horses bee pollen comment is an improved coat. The animals develop a full, thick, glossy coat that actually feels "bouncy" to the touch. Even in cold climates, the animals don't seem to mind the frigid temperatures, and their coats hold that nice summer shine.

These effects, as I already mentioned, have been well documented by researchers looking into the use of bee pollen by humans. But even without seeing the research papers that describe these results, many great trainers and breeders have been using the gifts from the bees to give their horses a boost into both better health and the winner's circle. If you aren't a regular at the track, you might still recognize a few of the names. The leader of the pollen-pack is Charlie Whittingham. Charlie has so many winners to his credit that it's hard to name them all. Whittingham is on the board of El Rancho Murrieta, near San Diego, California.

Other giants in the racing world that feed their horses bee pollen are Mel Studi, D. Wayne Lukas, Jack VanBerg, and Jim Maple. Jack Klugman (better known as an actor) is also getting into the act. As a licensed trainer and long-time consumer of bee pollen himself, it's a good bet that Klugman is serving his big stallion, Jackie Klugman, a heaping helping.

If you follow the Sport of Kings in all its different facets, you'll additionally be hearing about some up-and-comers, like the Willards down in Panama City, Florida, who specialize in quarter horses. William Shatner, of *Star Trek* fame, also feeds his quarter horses bee pollen.

COMMON MARKET

In lieu of reciting all the research facts and figures again, I'm giving you what scientists call a case study. A case study is a true tale. Mine is about a horse no one wanted. The horse's name is Common Market.

Common Market was picked up in a claiming race by W. Landolf of Mokena, Illinois, for the sum of $6,500. Claiming races are for horses whose owners are interested in selling. The track sets a purchase price that is applicable to every horse— winner or loser—in the race, and by paying an entry fee, a prospective buyer can pick up a good horse (or dog) at a bargain price. The animal, on the other hand, might turn out to be worthless. It's a gamble all the way. You pay your money and take your chances.

On June 20, 1987, Common Market ran last in a claiming race. Even worse, he was a known bleeder. Nevertheless, Landolf was committed. He claimed the bony gelding and took him home. His optimism faded as he looked over his purchase. All his worst fears were confirmed.

Common Market was apathetic and disinterested. When led, he barely lifted his hooves off the ground and merely plodded along, head down. In spite of the good care and good feed he was given during the first month after Landolf bought him, the horse ate little and steadily lost weight. His hair came out in the curry comb, and he looked terrible. His ribs were clearly visible. Landolf called in the vet and had Common Market wormed. He requested and got medication for the hair loss. But the usual treatments didn't help.

On July 16, 1987, Landolf started giving Common Market bee-pollen powder out of pure desperation. The horse refused to eat it. Certain that what he was about to do was right, Landolf mixed four ounces of powdered pollen with water and used a syringe to get it down the horse's throat. He continued the force-feeding procedure daily.

After ten days, Common Market was no longer losing weight and had even begun to gain. Landolf stopped force-feeding him and began mixing the bee pollen with feed. Common

Common Market on July 15, 1987, the day before he began receiving bee pollen.

Market's appetite returned full force, and he ate readily. He became more alert, too, and seemed more interested in what was going on around him.

Pictures don't lie. After one short month on bee pollen, Common Market had come a long way toward a healthier condition. His coat was thicker, and his ribs were barely visible any longer. It became obvious that the horse was no longer physically stressed.

After just forty-five days on supplemental bee pollen, Common Market had gained 200 pounds of much-needed weight. He was eating very well and taking in close to 12 quarts of grain mixed with bee pollen daily. His coat was sleek and shining, and no longer pulled out in the curry comb. His ears perked up when he heard something, and he took an interest in his surroundings. He stepped out smartly when ridden.

Soon, Common Market was feeling frisky. He started tossing his head and champing at the bit. It seemed he wanted to get going. On December 12, 1987, Landolf entered him in a race

Common Market on August 20, 1987, thirty-six days after he began eating bee-pollen-enriched feed.

and was pleased when he took second place. Landolf ran Common Market again on December 22, and again the horse finished second.

But it was the spring of 1988 that told the tale. On March 15, 1988, at Sportsman's Park in New Jersey, Common Market ran the six and a half furlongs and came home a winner. The following month, on April 28, 1988, he repeated his win on a mile romp, tail held high. Common Market was one happy horse. With barely a breather between the two races, he went a mile and sixteenth to win by a very impressive seven lengths. Common Market had come a roundabout trail to the winner's circle, but he had made it.

There is no doubt in Landolf's mind it was the bee pollen that caused the dramatic turnaround in Common Market. Landolf says, "Bee-pollen powder sure makes a difference. Just one look at the before, during, and after pictures of this great horse proves it." Thanks to Landolf's persistence in feeding the horse bee pollen, he was well repaid for his hunch. Common Market's

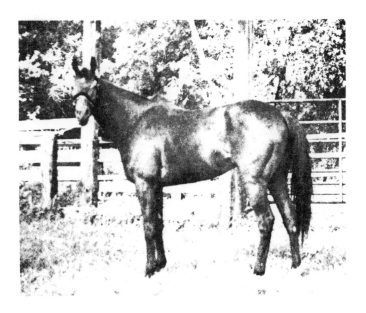

Common Market on September 13, 1987.

1988 winnings alone totaled $14,000. That $6,500 gamble Landolf took paid off—big.

SHOPPING FOR BEE PRODUCTS FOR HORSES

When shopping for supplements for your horses, please read labels carefully. It isn't just what's *in* a product that counts. What the manufacturer leaves *out* counts just as much, maybe more. I expect what you want for your horses are natural products from the beehive, formulations that contain no drugs, herbicides, pesticides, poisons, or toxic substances of any kind. Watch out for the non-nutrients, too—the unnecessary sugars, fillers, and additives.

When choosing supplements for your stock, know your source. Select products composed of natural food substances only. Products of this type are non-addictive and carry no contraindications of any kind. They may be fed at will without risk to the life and health of the animal. What you want are legal products that leave behind no traces of drugs or toxic substances, thus insuring that your horses will pass any spit box or test barn.

FEEDING FAMILY PETS

A growing body of evidence is showing that a lifetime of eating commercial pet foods can shorten your pet's life, can make him fatter than he should be, and can contribute to the development of such common disorders as diabetes, lead poisoning, rickets, sodium poisoning, and serious vitamin and mineral deficiencies, as well as cystitis and stones in cats and glaucoma and heart disease in dogs.

Statistics show pet owners in the United States spend over $10 billion every year on pet products. And still, with all our care and concern, we often don't do the right thing for these special members of the family. Remember, your pets are unable to communicate their nutritional needs. They are totally dependent on you.

Do you know what special nutrients your pet requires for life maintenance and good health? Briefly, your dog needs ten essential amino acids (proteins). They must be in properly balanced amounts to be efficiently utilized by your pet's digestive system. Another vital need is a high supply of methionine and triptophane. Dogs also need fatty acids, particularly linoleic, and choline for healthy metabolism. Linoleic acid is an excellent hair and skin conditioner. A dull, rough coat and dry, scaly skin are often the first signs of a serious vitamin and mineral deficiency.

Certain specific trace elements in minute amounts are essential for the catalytic action they provide in assisting many of your dog's internal functions. For example, to help your pet make full use of his regular diet, live enzymes and coenzymes are needed for healthy digestion. Research shows that the simple addition of the full range of digestive enzymes results in the utilization of up to *15 percent more* of the crude protein contained in commercial pet foods.

Cats, the other popular four-footed family members, require a higher concentration of essential nutrients than any other animal in the world, including man! Your cat requires eleven amino acids (proteins). These essential amino acids must be supplied in the diet. They are not manufactured within your cat's body.

Your cat must have a high supply of both calcium and phosphorus in perfectly balanced amounts. The fatty acids your kitty needs include linoleic and arachidonic. Vitamin C promotes an acid environment and can protect against cystitis, a common problem in cats. Feline cystitis can sometimes be fatal.

LOVE ISN'T ENOUGH

Americans are known worldwide for our deep love of the family pet. Yet, love isn't enough. Even worse, sometimes love for a pet is expressed as indulgence. Indulging our doggies and kitties means we often feed them too much, feed them the wrong foods, feed them exclusively on table scraps. You owe it to that loved and loving member of your family to make sure his nutritive needs are met.

According to R. G. Broderick, director of the Animal Clinic, Huntington, New York, "Almost all commercial pet foods fail to nourish a pet with special needs where vitamins are concerned. Many vitamins are killed during processing. If you feed your pets commercial diets, they will do better if you give them vitamin and mineral supplements."

Liebig's Law, an unchanging law of Nature first promulgated in the mid-1800s, teaches that *all* essential nutrients must be adequately represented in the diet in properly balanced amounts or the body cannot make efficient use of the elements it needs for healthy function. This basic truth applies to every animal on this sweet Earth, including man, and your pets as well.

Most of us know commercial pet foods are often lacking. With all the hullaballoo surrounding the people-oriented back-to-basics movement, there is currently growing pressure to improve pet foods as well. More and more of us are spending more and more dollars on better foods for family pets. Money talks, folks. Some of the giant pet-food processors are beginning to notice they are losing dollars and are altering their dog- and cat-food formulas accordingly.

King-A-Ling

King, a rangy Irish setter, came to the Antol family as a wobbly legged youngster. As large as he was, the big baby slept curled up at the foot of the bed of either of the two young sons in the family. In the mornings, King was up first. He toured the house, checked every room. If he was lucky, he found the family cat, a little black named Sukey, and coaxed her to play. When Sukey didn't care to chase or be chased, she preened herself out of reach on top of the refrigerator. After his morning outing with Papa Antol, King demanded his share of attention while the boys were dressing. Tug-of-war with a knotted sock was a favorite game. When the boys were young, it took both of them to hold the sock while the big dog tried to wrestle it from them.

King grew into a handsome and happy animal with a sleek and shining red coat. Soon, he discovered the female of the species. When King sniffed the air and scaled the fence, the family knew he was off to locate a mate. It was a good thing the big clown was a favorite in the neighborhood. He was impossible to catch when he was on the trail. You may not believe it, but—the family swears it's the truth—when the boys and Papa Antol came home exhausted from the chase, Mama Antol would send Sukey out to bring King home. Within an hour, the little black cat and the big red dog would come trotting home side by side.

As the years ticked by, King's muzzle became gray and grizzled, but his happy disposition and devotion to the family never wavered. With the help of a vet, he was nursed through hip dysplasia, a condition common to his breed. In spite of the love and care lavished on him, the day came when the old gentleman could no longer make it up onto the boys' beds. He slept instead in his big wicker dog bed, cozy and soft with blankets.

There were still more trials awaiting this dog and the family that loved him. King was getting very old, and the family was worried. Although he didn't seem to be in pain, he had a great deal of difficulty getting around and often had to be helped to his feet. An appointment was made with the vet. King had always enjoyed a bath and brushing, but now he was no longer eager for a grooming. As Mama Antol

King

combed out his long silky hair, she felt a series of hard lumps deep under his skin. The vet confirmed that King was suffering from widespread, deep-seated cancer and recommended he be put to sleep. The family couldn't bear to put down their old friend without making an all-out effort to save him.

The family had all been taking bee pollen for a long time and were big fans of the product. Mama Antol began sprinkling a liberal handful of pollen on top of the special food prescribed by the vet. At first, King sniffed the granules and licked them off the top. After a few days, he ate some bites of food along with the pollen. Within a month, the stiffness in his hindquarters seemed to have lessened, and he was eating a full serving of food. After two months, although he wasn't frisking around like a puppy, he was more like his old self and his appetite had come back. It was hard to tell, but it looked as if his cancerous lumps were getting smaller as well.

Then the day came when the family found King up on a bed. The family cheered and fussed over him, petted him, and called him "good dog." They were certain the worst had passed, and they were right. Once again, King enjoyed his walks. He never took off at the scent of a female again, but he padded alongside a family member contentedly when taken out and still stopped to investigate an interesting tree or two along the way.

For a full two years after the crisis that almost took King from them, the Antol family cared for and loved the aging animal. That love was returned in full measure. Then the time came when King just couldn't make it outside. The old gentleman looked embarrassed and whined an apology when he wet his bed. His back legs had given out completely. He could no longer drag himself to his feet.

Not willing to allow their beloved old friend to suffer, the family agreed with wet eyes that King's time had come. Because King had always hated the trip to the doctor, Mama Antol phoned the vet and arranged a house call for a time when everyone was out of the house. With much love, she hoisted the now-fragile animal to the bed, wrapped him lovingly in his blankets, and kissed him goodbye. She stroked his head, breathed a prayer, and hugged him close while the vet administered the lethal injection. With a gentle sigh, the great dog closed his eyes and slept the good sleep forever.

King was 15 years old, the equivalent of 105 human years. He had lived an extraordinarily long and very full life for his breed. The family is certain bee pollen inhibited and controlled the cancer that had invaded his body, allowed him to overcome the stiffness of arthritis that made it so difficult for him to move, and restored him to a measure of health. King lived a happy and contented two full years beyond the time allotted him by his doctor.

Needless to say, all the many Antol family pets that followed King—and at one time the family had six dogs and three cats—are given dietary bee pollen from the time they join the household.

SHOPPING FOR BEE PRODUCTS FOR PETS

In the meantime, you might want to supplement your pet's diet directly with bee-pollen granules or with those special nutrient-rich natural formulas that incorporate the products of the hive.

Sources of good dietary pet supplements include your local

health-food store, your vet, and a good pet shop. Most supermarkets have a special section devoted to pets. Before making
your selection, check the label. For your pet, as for yourself,
please select low-sodium supplements (and foods) without
unnecessary processing chemicals or toxic substances of any
kind. Pass up supplements (and foods) containing dyes and
artificial colorings. Dyes are not only non-nutrients, they are
unnecessary and some can be toxic. Other non-nutrients include sugars, fillers, and additives.

Here's a good rule of thumb: If you wouldn't take the ingredients of a supplement (or processed food) yourself, don't give
them to your pet.

8

THE APIARIAN LIFESTYLE

An ancient Oriental greeting of great courtesy, always accompanied by a deep bow, is the phrase "May you live a thousand years." I think the Apiarian Lifestyle may be the key to the Chinese puzzle of the millennial lifestyle—living one thousand years!

In this chapter, I'm going to let you in on the Apiarian Lifestyle. I'm convinced this way of living is what is keeping me young, healthy, and working hard in my seventies. I'm equally convinced it will work for you, too.

I'm not a true vegetarian. In general, strict vegetarians do not eat anything that once had a heartbeat, including poultry and seafoods, nor their products, such as milk and eggs. There is a subcategory that further differentiates a certain type of vegetarian. Lacto-ovo vegetarians do not eat animal flesh but do consume dairy products, signified by the term "lacto" (Latin for "milk"), and eggs, signified by the term "ovo" (Latin for "egg").

I have appropriated the title of World's Number-One Apiarian. Because I coined the term, I guess there's no one to challenge me just yet. "Apiarian" is a term I originated to describe my lifestyle. I do eat certain types of dairy products, do eat certain kinds of eggs, and do eat some meat. "Apiarian," of course, comes from "apiary," which is where bees are kept. "Apiary" comes from "Apis mellifera," the domestic honeybee that produces all those miraculous products mankind prizes. The products of the beehive—bee pollen, bee propolis, royal jelly, and honey—are the basic staples of my diet.

THE APIARIAN PHILOSOPHY

Apiarianism is a very fulfilling lifestyle. It is based on health—eating the most healthy foods, doing health-promoting activities, holding healthy beliefs. When you live healthy, being healthy follows.

I have developed—and live—six basic apiarian precepts. They are broad categories that cover my life. I am proud to share them with you. I am very healthy. My wife and children are healthy. I would very much like you to be healthy. My basic apiarian precepts, which I strongly believe are the reason for my extraordinary health, are as follows:

- Apiarians eat the most healthful, totally organic foods possible. Because bee pollen offers all the nutrients necessary for life, it may be the only perfect food on Earth. I enjoy the products of the beehive with each and every meal every day.

- Complete apiarians engage in at least one hour of strenuous exercise five days per week. The exercise regimen should bring on a continuous and healthy cleansing sweat for the duration of the session.

- Apiarians enjoy a regular sleep pattern, with five, six, or seven hours of uninterrupted sleep each night. Successful apiarians peacefully pass into deep fifth-stage slumber, the most healthy and restful sleep of all.

- The Apiarian Lifestyle helps individuals completely manage any stressful situation they may encounter during the day. Fully evolved apiarians effortlessly transform daily stress from a destroying force in their lives into a potentiating and building force.

- Apiarians enjoy warm and active sexual relationships with their chosen lifetime partners. Satisfying sexual experiences are a wholesome and welcome part of the Apiarian Lifestyle.

- True apiarianism cannot be fully experienced unless the individual has a personal relationship with the Supreme Being, no matter what name the Supreme Being is called in the particular faith. That name may be God, Christ, Yahweh, Jehovah, or something else. High-level apiarians have perfect faith.

I have stated my precepts here in abbreviated form. They look simple this way. They are simple. In the first half of this chapter, I'm going to explain them more fully and show you how I interpret them for myself. Then you can really see how simple they are and how easy it would be for you to slide them into your life.

Pick and choose. You don't have to incorporate every one right away. You don't even have to incorporate them all, although the more you do, the better. Good luck. See you at the end of the millennium!

ORGANIC NUTRITION

Don't be fooled. Don't be misled by the simplistic saying, "All you need to do to consume all the nutrients your body requires is to eat balanced meals from the four basic food groups." That fairy tale might have been honored once upon a time, but today it is considered dangerous nonsense.

Why? If you've been paying attention, I think you already know why. In Chapter 3, I discussed all those studies by the United States Department of Agriculture (USDA) that showed not one state in the United States still has all the natural nutrients present in its soil. Then, too, there's all those poisonous agribiz chemicals commercial food growers till in their fields and dust on their crops. Here's irrefutable proof that American consumers are in trouble:

- The USDA has determined that 35 to 37 percent of the food eaten by the average American family is manmade. Manmade foods cannot legitimately be categorized in any one of the four basic food groups.

- In 1987, the USDA surveyed the food intake of 21,000 average Americans to find out if they were consuming 100 percent of the Recommended Daily Allowance (RDA) of ten essential nutrients. Not one person among the entire 21,000 studied—*not one*—was consuming a diet that provided the RDA of the targeted ten essential nutrients.

The only possible conclusion to be reached from these disturbing statistics is that the essential nutrients are not present in the foods in our supermarkets. Surely, if sufficient nutrients were available in commercially grown and processed foods to permit consumption of the RDA of ten essential nutrients, at least 100, or 10, or even 1 person in that study of 21,000 would have tested positive regarding the RDA requirements.

This USDA study proved that the average American family eating supermarket food is eating a less-than-adequate diet for healthy functioning.

Processed Manmade Foods

"Never eat any food man has tampered with to make a profit." This truism comes from the supergreat Victor Earl Irons, a personal friend who is in his nineties and who is the greatest fighter for our health freedoms I know.

By and large, any of the manufactured and processed so-called foods advertised on television are a no-no. Virtually all of the food products so colorfully and artfully advertised on television are manmade for one reason: to make a profit.

If the manufactured food products in the supermarket do not provide the essential nutrients, and they do not, what's the solution?

Organically Grown Foods

You already know the products of the beehive are organic powerhouses of nutrients. What exactly are organically grown foods? There are many definitions of such foods, but here's the way I define them: Organically grown foodstuffs are those foods grown in soil that contains an abundance of Mother Nature's cultivators, earthworms. Living worms cannot survive in chemically treated soil. Artificial, chemical fertilizers, pesticides, and herbicides—manmade poisons all—drive earthworms away or kill them. If no earthworms are in soil, the foodstuffs grown in that soil are probably nutrient-deficient, almost certainly contaminated with chemicals. Earthworms are God's environmentalists. If there's an abundance of earthworms in soil, you can be certain the soil is organic, and the produce grown in that soil can be accurately termed organically grown.

Apiarians strive to eat only organic, nutrient-rich foods. The best foods I know in each category are as follows:

- General—the products of the beehive.
- Meats—raw veal liver.
- Fowl—raw fertile eggs.
- Fish—cod-liver oil.
- Dairy—raw goat's milk and raw-goat's-milk cheese.
- Fruits—raw mangoes.
- Vegetables—raw carrots and raw leafy greens.
- Grains—millet.
- Cereals—buckwheat, rye, and oats.
- Nuts—almonds.
- Seeds—flax, pumpkin, sesame, alfalfa, and chia.
- Oils—flax seed and pumpkin seed.

Other foods in each category are also excellent. For example, all raw vine- or tree-ripened fruits are superb. However, the foods above are the best, and I'll discuss them more fully in the following pages.

Note: Let me just inject something here concerning my preferences for *raw* veal liver, *raw* fertile eggs, and *raw* milk and cheese. These are my *personal* preferences. If you choose to eat these foods, you must take into account all the warnings about food poisoning, including salmonella poisoning, due to the bacteria generally present in raw foods and the spoilage prompted by the difficulty in storing and preserving raw food items. I eat these foods with my eyes wide open. These foods are part of my *personal* lifestyle, and what I am doing here is describing my personal lifestyle. How you live your life, including which foods you eat, must be your personal choice.

Now, on to my personal best food choices.

General

In prior chapters, I told you a great deal about the products of the beehive, but here's a brief review. Bee pollen is rightly called the world's perfect food because it contains all the nutrients necessary to sustain life. Propolis is the source of the most powerful natural antibiotic yet discovered. Because it also has antiseptic, antibacterial, and antiviral properties, propolis qualifies as Mother Nature's premiere preventive. Royal jelly is rich in hormonal factors and supernutrients. The royal milk also contains some mysterious factor that extends the life span and retards the aging process.

Meats

In the meats category, raw veal liver is the best food I know. Consider this: When a lion or tiger kills an animal, the first part of the flesh it consumes is the liver. I believe the lion and tiger know more about nutrition than any person walking the Earth. The predatory big cats know the liver is the most nutritious part of an animal. They instinctively consume the liver first because it is the most invigorating food and contains the most-needed nutrients.

I buy very fresh raw veal liver from certified all-organic beef, which is raised cleanly without chemicalized feed, antibiotics, or hormone injections. Again, however, if you choose to consume raw veal liver, or raw meat of any kind, you must be aware of the possible consequences, that is, food poisoning.

Fowl

To my way of thinking, raw *fertile* eggs are the best food from this group. The life cycle of the chicken, duck—any bird—begins in the egg. Each raw fertile egg contains the life force of one living thing. When that egg is eaten raw, I believe, it is one of the best foods humans can ingest.

I don't worry about the cholesterol content of eggs. The Creator doesn't make mistakes. There is an abundance of fat-emulsifying lecithin in the yolk of an egg. It is only when the egg is cooked that the lecithin loses its ability to emulsify fat and the cholesterol content of the egg becomes dangerous. Lecithin is heat sensitive. Cooking damages it.

However, once more, you must be very, very careful when you eat a raw egg. You must be sure of your source, and you must also make sure the egg is very fresh. There have been cases of salmonella poisoning recently in persons who have eaten raw or even lightly cooked eggs. Cooking destroys the salmonella bacteria that may be lurking in a raw egg.

Fish

According to research, Grandmother was right when she routinely spooned a dose of cod-liver oil into the mouth of every member of the family every day. Because I believe it to be the best food in the fish category, I still take cod-liver oil. I swig down a mouthful once or twice a week.

Dairy

Apiarians eat all dairy products together at one meal, preferably breakfast. I enjoy acidophilus goat's milk along with one to four ounces of goat cheese. The goat cheese I buy is raw, unpasteurized, and unhomogenized. I prefer the Swiss type. According to Dr. Bernard Jensen, the greatest healer and health authority I know, the best source of goat cheese and goat whey is the Mt. Capra Cheese company of Chehalis, Washington (see the Source List, page 201).

Apiarians regulate their personal intake of dairy products to suit their particular lifestyle and requirements.

Fruits

All organically grown fruits are good food. Apiarians eat fully ripe fruits, preferably ripened on the vine or tree. Unripe fruits are difficult to digest, and green fruits don't offer the full nutrient value of ripe fruits. In addition, apiarians are not satisfied to merely drink the juice of a fruit but eat the whole fruit, taking care to chew each bite thoroughly. As a rule of thumb, bypass fruit juices and enjoy Nature's bounty in its nutrient-rich whole form.

Start adding fruits to your menu slowly, until you can comfortably enjoy one all-fruit meal daily during the summer months, when the sweet harvest is vine- or tree-ripened and fresh. But try to avoid citrus fruits. Their acid content can be upsetting to the stomach. In spite of their touted vitamin-C content, I believe citrus fruits to be the least desirable of all fruits.

To my way of thinking, the best of all fruits is the mango, often called the king of fruits not only because of its superior taste but for its superior nutrient content. The watermelon closely follows in nutrient value.

Vegetables

All vegetables are excellent foods for apiarians as long as they come from organically rich soil. Juiced vegetables are also excellent. Green, leafy vegetables are especially good for juicing.

Cruciferous vegetables (cabbage, cauliflower, and broccoli) have been shown to have anticancer properties. Orange vegetables provide beta-carotene, which the body uses to manufacture vitamin A. Beta-carotene is another documented cancer preventive that belongs on apiarians' menus. (By the way, it shouldn't come as a surprise that bee pollen contains by weight twenty times more beta-carotene than carrots do.)

Grains

Millet is the best grain I know. It is not only rich in phosphorus, a necessary companion of calcium, but it also contains nitrilosides. According to Dr. Bernard Jensen, nitrilosides help inhibit the growth of cancer cells. Scientists point to the low rate of cancer in primitive societies where unrefined foods rich in nitrilosides are eaten daily.

Cereals

The cereals I personally favor are buckwheat, rye, and oats. You know, of course, that I'm talking about minimally processed cereals, not the refined and overprocessed cereals you find in your supermarket. Like millet, buckwheat is rich in nitrilosides. Rye encourages the development of a lean, muscular body. Oats—indeed, all the cereal grains—are rich in fiber.

Are you looking in vain for wheat? You won't find it on my list. In spite of its good reputation, wheat causes problems for many people. A hidden allergy or sensitivity to wheat is more common than you might think.

Nuts

Almonds are on the apiarian's must-eat list. Dr. Bernard Jensen says almonds are the "king of nuts, being highest in alkalinity." You might be surprised to learn that one cup of raw almonds contains 332 milligrams of calcium. Edgar Cayce, the psychic healer, was also a great advocate of almonds. According to Cayce, eating almonds daily protects against cancer.

Seeds

Because seeds contain the life force of a plant, all raw seeds, including chia seeds, are rich in proteins, micronutrients, and trace elements. Alfalfa is also rich in cleansing chlorophyll and helps normalize bowel action. On top of all their other nutrients, flax and pumpkin seeds offer the essential fatty acids (EFAs), elements the body needs daily and can't manufacture internally. You'll learn more about the EFAs in the Oils category.

Oils

The best foods in this category seem to be flax seed oil and pumpkin seed oil. However, chances are that neither has an honored place on your family table. Yet flax seed oil is acknowledged as the world's most abundant source of the essential fatty acids.

The EFAs, linoleic and linolenic, are medically termed essential because the body cannot synthesize them from any other nutrient or combination of nutrients. Linoleic and linolenic fatty acids are required by many internal systems. For life support, they must be supplied to the body daily. If they are deficient, the body attempts to compensate for them, sometimes for many years. When a serious illness strikes, a nutrient deficiency is seldom pinpointed as a contributing factor and often escapes unnoticed. Unfortunately, for the most part, the EFAs have been processed out of the American diet.

When investigating the properties of the EFAs, research scientists the world over use flax seed oil in their clinical tests. Studies show dramatically that flax seed oil is both a preventive and an active therapeutic agent. For example, Polish scientists have shown that the EFAs destroy cancer cells without harming the vital white blood cells of the immune system. In Britain, medical detectives showed that even when fed a grossly high-fat diet, subjects protected by flax seed oil were free of the harmful elements that develop in the blood when fats can't be processed by the body. Australian researchers demonstrated that dangerously high blood pressure is reduced in subjects supplied regularly with the EFAs.

But the strongest proof of all comes from Dr. Johanna Budwig, Germany's premiere biochemist. Dr. Budwig showed in the late 1970s and early 1980s that the blood of seriously ill and diseased persons always exhibits very low levels of linoleic acid. She found that healthy blood always contains both of the EFAs along with quality proteins. Diseased blood does not.

Without the vital marriage of the EFAs and sulfur-based proteins, the production of hemoglobin (oxygen-carrying red blood cells) is impaired. Cells and tissues suffer from oxygen deprivation.

In over a decade of clinical application, Dr. Budwig has been successfully treating victims of the diseases of fatty degeneration with a dietary therapy focusing on unrefined flax seed oil and protein-rich, low-fat cottage cheese. She has put into practice what laboratory studies have proven: once the body is provided with the EFAs and the nutrients needed to process them, it can very often work internal corrections and restore itself to health.

Because it is a true cold-pressed, unrefined flax oil from the first pressing of the seeds, BioSan Flax Seed Oil is the brand I favor. Major health-food stores carry it, and it has been endorsed by Dr. Budwig herself.

Pumpkin seed oil is also a good source of the EFAs. However, it is not as rich or as well balanced overall as flax seed oil.

The Forbidden List

Among the items on the Forbidden List when following the Apiarian Lifestyle are pork, shellfish, hydrogenated and partially hydrogenated fats and oils, alcohol, coffee, tea (except caffeine-free herbal teas), cola and other carbonated beverages, and tobacco.

A prime directive for apiarians is never to eat any animal that feeds on decaying dead matter or the droppings of other animals. Called scavengers, they include the pig and shellfish, such as crab, lobster, shrimp, and oysters. Shellfish grow plump by feeding on the bottom of seabeds.

Consuming scavenging animals is forbidden by many religions. In addition, scientific research shows people should not eat the meat of scavenging creatures because of the difficulty in digesting it; it knocks the metabolism out of kilter.

Also on the Forbidden List are chemically altered dietary fats. Over half (57 percent) of the fats in the American diet come from manmade, commercially processed fats and oils, such as vegetable oil, margarine, salad dressing, and shortening. All nutrients have been processed out of these dead, non-nutritive fats. Hydrogenated and partially hydrogenated fats contain alien metabolites. Many, including some packaged in plastic, contain harmful chemicals.

Start reading labels and you'll discover hydrogenated and partially hydrogenated fats are in just about every manufactured food product in the supermarket. Yet they are impossible for the body to process properly. Many authorities cite research showing these chemically altered fats lay the foundation for the diseases of fatty degeneration, including heart disease and cancer. These dead, artificial dietary fats have been clinically shown to be harmful to the body.

Liquifying Your Food

Most people eat entirely too fast, barely tasting their food before taking the next bite. For perfect digestion and assimilation, apiarians chew their food until the solids have become liquified. This is a very difficult challenge to master. However, I believe perfect health cannot be achieved without consistently liquifying the bites of solid food you put in your mouth. Some people call this process fletcherizing, a procedure that calls for chewing your food at least thirty times before swallowing.

You may find it difficult to always fletcherize your food. But, if overweight apiarians completely liquify every bite of solid food, they will lose weight in a consistent and systematic way, gradually achieving their perfect weight. It is a medical fact that twenty minutes, on average, must pass before your stomach signals your brain that you have eaten enough. This rule applies whether you shovel in massive amounts and swallow rapidly or you systematically liquify each bite.

Apiarians eat slowly. After each bite, put your fork back on your plate. Continue chewing methodically until that bite has been completely liquified. Fletcherize every bite you take and, very soon, you will find you have developed another life-extending habit.

"Chewing" Your Liquids

When apiarians drink goat's milk or any other liquid, they swish each sip around in their mouth and "chew" it from eight to fifteen times to completely mix it with the digestive juices present in saliva. Chewing begins the digestive process so necessary for good digestion and assimilation.

Water

Apiarians never drink water from a public water supply. Municipalities artificially chlorinate and fluoridate the water that comes from your tap. Chlorine kills cells, injures red blood cells, and interferes with blood pressure. Chlorinated water cannot be used in kidney dialysis machines because of these harmful internal actions.

Fluoride is a poisonous by-product of aluminum manufacture. It is often used as rat poison. It has been scientifically confirmed in worldwide research that persons who drink fluoridated water have a higher death rate from all causes, cancer in particular, than those who drink pure water. Both the USSR and Japan have banned the use of fluoride in public water supplies as well as by dentists.

To purify your water, invest in a home water-purification system. The only purifying system that works perfectly is reverse osmosis. In this method of purification, tap water is forced through a semipermeable membrane. The microscopic holes in the semipermeable membrane permit the passage of only hydrogen and oxygen molecules. All harmful chemicals, contaminants, pollutants, asbestos, and lead—and chlorine and fluoride—are separated out and flushed down the drain into the sewer, where they belong. The result is an unlimited flow of perfectly pure water.

Virtually all water-purification systems denude the water of important trace minerals. Jeffrey Bland, Ph.D., says approximately 25 percent of the total mineral intake of mankind comes from the water we drink. I personally replace the trace minerals lost from my purified water by adding MiVita Minerals, a mineral water (see the Source List, page 201), at the rate of one tablespoon or more per gallon.

Elimination

This is not a very tasteful subject, but it is important. Regulating the digestive tract to achieve perfect elimination is often glossed over by health authorities. Yet, checking your feces is the best way to tell what's going on internally in your body. Here's what to look for:

Healthy fecal matter will be one to one-and-a-half inches in diameter and approximately twelve to fifteen inches long. Fresh, healthy feces float. Generally speaking, evacuated feces will be connected. However, you can expect to find the matter broken, as it usually comes apart upon hitting the water in the toilet bowl.

Healthy feces will be a yellowish or brownish color. The smell should not be offensive. At most, the odor should not be strong enough to be repulsive. A slightly sour odor indicates the presence of hydrochloric acid, normal in healthy feces.

If your intestines are full of putrifying matter, which is indicated by unhealthy (hard, dry, fractured, runny, smelly) feces, then your gastrointestinal tract is not working efficiently. If you have a digestive-tract problem, you may be lacking lactobacillus acidophilus. Acidophilus is a necessary, friendly bacterium that normally lives in the body.

A healthy body has a healthy supply of acidophilus bacillus. Acidophilus has been identified as a powerful enemy of undesirable bacterial strains as well as *Candida albicans*. Candida, which causes the common yeast infection, is kept under control by acidophilus.

Many internal systems rely on acidophilus for healthy functioning. Everything from chronic diarrhea, gastrointestinal upsets (with accompanying gas attacks and flatulence), common vaginal yeast infections, and low energy levels to canker sores and fever blisters (herpes simplex virus) yield to an influx of lactobacillus acidophilus.

A healthy gastrointestinal tract is plentifully supplied with acidophilus, but the normal amount of this helpful bacterium is quickly wiped out by antibiotics and hormone therapy. If you have been on a course of antibiotics, chances are you need dietary acidophilus.

Fortunately, it's relatively easy to re-establish a depleted acidophilus colony. Your health-food store has various sources of acidophilus, from liquids to capsules. Just be sure to select a brand that guarantees a high content of live bacteria. Yes, yogurt contains acidophilus, but different brands offer different amounts. Frozen, sweetened yogurts are generally very low in this necessary bacterium. You really can't rely solely on yogurt to replenish acidophilus.

I keep my body well supplied with acidophilus by drinking acidophilus-enriched goat's milk in my Breakfast Bacillus every morning. A little later in this chapter, you'll find my personal recipe for this clabbered (curdled) goat's milk. This fortified breakfast drink provides the entire gastrointestinal tract with billions of bacteria that happily take up residence on the walls of the intestines. In spite of a daily drink of these friendly live spores, however, it may take beginning apiarians up to six months to achieve perfect elimination.

By examining their stools each morning, apiarians will notice the condition of their fecal matter progressing toward perfection, showing digestion and assimilation are improving with each "passing" day.

Do It Now

When peristalsis begins and your body signals your bowels need emptying, never wait. Always answer the call immediately. Bowel elimination is best accomplished at Nature's urging. Evacuation is more thorough when the first urge arises.

One reason why the so-called primitive peoples of the world enjoy such good health is that they are completely uninhibited about their bodily functions. When Nature calls, they may even make a deposit by the side of the road. No one thinks them crude or rude. Evacuating the bowels is a natural, healthy function.

EXERCISE EXTENDS THE LIFE SPAN

It has been medically and scientifically documented that exercising regularly increases longevity and enhances the quality of life as well. This fact has been confirmed in worldwide studies so many times that it is impossible to refute. I work out with weights, swim, skip rope, and run.

On November 6, 1988, I ran in the New York City Marathon for the first time, finishing the entire distance of 26 miles 385 yards 2 feet. I was seventy-one at the time. I ran with Noel Johnson, then eighty-nine (see page 111). Thanks in no small part to his fondness for the products of the beehive, Johnson seems to grow younger each year. He holds the North American record for senior marathoners. During this marathon, I also met Manning Wein of Van Nuys, California. Then eighty-six, Wein qualified as the second-oldest marathoner of record.

People who have not been exercising on a regular basis must see their doctor to make sure their physical condition will permit them to engage in a daily exercise program. If your doctor gives the okay, you can begin an exercise regimen.

All authorities emphasize that people beginning an exercise program should start at a slow pace and work up to their optimum level. A word of caution is in order here. Nearly everyone who begins exercising is overenthusiastic, pushing beyond healthy limits at first. Starting out with a walking-jogging program is advisable. As your strength and confidence build, ease into running. If you can manage to run only fifty steps before feeling tired, that's just fine. Stop. The following day, you might run sixty steps before pooping out.

Skipping Rope

Boxers routinely skip rope to develop their leg muscles and enhance the balance and coordination they need to dance around the ring. The most strenuous single exercise I know is skipping rope with the feet together on a fast, continuous basis. This exercise accelerates the heart rate, causing the entire body to pulsate. It gives me a maximum workout.

*Skipping rope gives me
a maximum workout.*

Running

For me, the next-best exercise is running *up*stairs or *up*hill. Running on a level surface is probably the type of exercise that suits most physically active people. I run as fast as I can for one hour three days per week. Two days per week, I work out with weights. I also swim laps five evenings per week.

Let's face it, folks. Running is boring. That's probably why a lot of people who enthusiastically take up running drop it after a month or two. I've worked out some tricks to eliminate the boredom of running alone.

Run the same path every morning. Carry a stopwatch. Time yourself as you pass certain designated landmarks along the way. You'll be surprised at how exhilarating and encouraging it is to find you've cut a second or two off your previous time as you speed past the fireplug in the middle of the block, then reach the big tree in the park. On the homestretch, hustle around the corner past the gray house with the black shutters. Give yourself a mental cheer on finding you're three seconds ahead of your best previous time. You get the idea.

Remember, you aren't competing with anyone but yourself. Of course, once you get really fast, you might want to enter a 10K (ten-kilometer race). After you build stamina and endurance, you might want to run a marathon to test yourself against some real competition. However, that shouldn't be the goal of your exercise program. What apiarians aim for is their personal best, running as closely as possible to their maximum capacity while sustaining the pace for an entire hour.

Don't overdo any type of exercise until your body is accustomed to an exercise regimen. Nathan Pritikin once told me it took him five years to work up to running an hour as fast as he could every day. He said he was afraid of having a heart attack the entire time.

Perhaps five years is too long to "ease" into an exercise program. However, I do advise you to increase your time and speed gradually instead of trying to run all-out for an hour right away. A year would not be too long.

I thoroughly enjoy competing with myself. I like pumping uphill and working up a sweat. For me, running is the greatest. However, there's another form of exercise that also gives tremendous physical results but without such hard work.

Rebounding

A rebound-exercise device is a personal-sized home version of a trampoline. The best are round, about three feet in diameter, and about nine inches high. Because it needs to be very resilient and shouldn't sag or bag, the best bouncing surface is made of a material called Permatron.

Rebounding combines the forces of acceleration and deceleration to fool the cells of the body into believing they are being subjected to increased gravity. That's the secret of the rebound's success.

It is a medical fact that every cell in the body adjusts immediately to its environment. When astronauts travel in space at zero gravity, they lose bone density and muscle mass very quickly. Using blood samples from returning American astronauts and Soviet cosmonauts, scientists subjected weakened blood cells to an increase in G-force (gravitational force). The cells responded by becoming stronger than they were under normal Earth gravity. Even the white blood cells of the immune system included in the blood samples were dramatically strengthened. The National Aeronautics and Space Administration (NASA) has established that rebounding is 68 percent more efficient than running.

When you first step onto a rebounder and begin bouncing, you'll notice you feel heavier at the bottom of a bounce when you are in the deceleration mode. That's the increased G-force that challenges all the cells in your body to become stronger.

The real beauty of rebounding is that it can be custom tailored to the age and condition of the individual. Unlike running, which requires real physical stamina, no one is too old or too infirm to benefit from rebounding. Even a patient in a wheelchair can rest his feet on the bouncing surface while a partner does the bounding. The effect will travel from the soles of the resting feet through the entire body.

For my money, the best rebounder around is the Dynabound, engineered by Albert Earl Carter. This one won't let you down in midbounce. Carter is acknowledged internationally as the world's foremost authority on rebound exercise. He is the author of *The New Miracles of Rebound Exercise* and *The Cancer Answer*. For where to find the books, see the Source List, page 201.

TO SLEEP, PERCHANCE TO DREAM

REM, short for "rapid eye movement," signals the sleeper is dreaming and has entered the stage of deep sleep. Fifth-stage slumber, or REM sleep, is the most healthy and restorative of life energies. The contribution that deep sleep plays in keeping us well and energetic is often overlooked. The sleep that comes in the fifth stage is such a restful, healing sleep, it is actually rejuvenating.

Unfortunately, many people never receive the full restorative benefits of deep sleep. They are restless, sleep fitfully, and remain in the third level of sleep the entire night. These are the people who wonder why they always awaken grouchy and still tired.

The best way to coax your body into progressing naturally into fifth-stage slumber is to practice complete relaxation. No matter which method or regimen you use to accomplish this, complete relaxation of the entire body is what sets the stage for healthy REM sleep.

You cannot enter fifth-stage slumber unless your stomach is empty. For four hours before retiring, don't eat. About 75 percent of your entire blood supply is used to digest food in your stomach. You want that blood busy repairing body tissue, not digesting food, while you are sleeping.

People who regularly reach fifth-stage slumber sleep deeply and awaken refreshed and raring to go. These people need less sleep-hours than others because their body is benefiting fully from their slumber each night, as Nature intended.

Upon retiring and fully relaxing all your muscles, clear your mind of the cares of the day. Focus on something pleasant. To drift off to dreamland effortlessly, practice deep breathing from the abdomen. Passing into fifth-stage slumber will occur naturally. This may not happen the first time you try, but it will happen in time. Once you experience the full effects and restful benefits of deep sleep, you will marvel at the difference you feel on awakening in the morning.

The restorative and rejuvenating benefits of fifth-stage slumber are incalculable. Believe it.

MANAGING STRESS

The hectic pace of the modern world makes stress unavoidable. A loved one is seriously ill. There's a traffic jam on the way to work. The boss is a bear. A thorny decision is required, but no matter what you decide, someone will be left disgruntled. The car needs repair. Funds are low. The kids are cranky. Your mate is cross. There's too much that needs doing and not enough time to do it all. Rush, rush, rush. Wrong. Wrong. Wrong.

Slow down. Relax. Meditate a moment. Put must-do's in priority order. Take first things first. Clearing the mind while clearing the decks for action may be all that's necessary to evaporate the stress we all feel when there's too much on our plates. Take a few deep cleansing breaths. Deep abdominal breathing is excellent against destructive stress. So is exercise. Work off that surge of adrenalin in a workout.

Stress is part of life. Stress can be destructive or beneficial. Whether it is harmful is largely up to you. Once you make up your mind to take things as they come and handle problems calmly, the daily challenges you face can become invigorating instead of enervating.

Apiarians accept circumstances as they arise. Change for the better those you can, but accept those you can't alter. Always strive to "live and let live." Be philosophic. By next week, most of the stress of today will be only a dim memory if you treat it as such.

SEXUAL FUNCTION

I believe sex is a dynamic and necessary part of life that is mishandled by many people. To my way of thinking, sex is the perfect way for both men and women to start the day relaxed and ready for any problems that may arise. It's one of the best stressbusters around, too.

Because of the way the male body reacts, it seems logical to assume the Creator probably meant men to have sex first thing in the morning. When they wake up, men are rested. They normally awaken with an erection. Women also awaken rested. A couple is lying together side-by-side in bed. What a perfect time to have sex.

By the way, I don't believe the Creator meant sex for procreation only. If that were true, men and women would lose their sex drive once they were no longer able to reproduce. I am in my seventies and, I assure you, my sex drive is alive and well.

This apiarian thinks men and women should have sexual intercourse every day, first thing in the morning. With the help of the hormone-charged products of the bee, there's no reason why this pleasurable regimen should not continue for a lifetime. The Apiarian Lifestyle insures it.

PERFECT FAITH

I don't believe perfect health can be achieved without a personal relationship with the Supreme Being. In itself, an abiding faith can overcome and eliminate stress. Deep personal faith helps everyone function better in every department.

President Dwight D. Eisenhower said of himself, "I must be a Christian." Eisenhower said being a good Christian required 10 percent of his money and 10 percent of his time and enjoined him to do the right thing at all times, which he said he felt he should do anyway. He confided that a lack of belief in a Higher Power and the possibility of being mistaken at life's end were so horrible that he couldn't afford the risk.

If the alternative faced by nonbelievers is eternal damnation, apiarians must be devout followers of their personal religion.

Religious wars and interdenominational controversy seem foolish to me. All faiths acknowledge one Supreme Being. No matter what name the Creator is given in one faith or another, no matter how learned or devout a person may be, no one knows for sure just how the hereafter is constructed.

It seems to me there's one great truth running through all religions. If an individual doesn't live an exemplary life here on Earth, his chances of enjoying the hereafter will necessarily be curtailed, reduced, even eliminated altogether. I believe a sinful-living, carousing, gluttonous person on Earth will not be rewarded in the hereafter.

MY APIARIAN LIFESTYLE

What I've given you so far in this chapter are general guidelines. Everyone should adapt the Apiarian Lifestyle to suit his personal timetable. I'm not a doctor. I can't write out a prescription for you to follow. But I can tell you exactly what works for me.

My lifestyle evolved over a period of years, undergoing some fine-tuning along the way. Yes, it was difficult in the beginning. It takes strong physical and mental self-discipline to live healthy, but the rewards are great. With the hope that others may be encouraged to make some changes for the better in their lifestyles, here's a review of the regimen I've been practicing for perhaps fifteen to twenty years now.

MY DAILY REGIMEN

At the dawn of time and really till just a few centuries ago, man was awake and active only during the sunlit hours. He slept through the dark hours of the night. That's the way man's body was designed to operate.

As artificial lighting became common, the cycle changed. We discovered how important sunlight is to health during the Industrial Revolution. As families left the farms and adults began working under artificial lighting in factories, men and women often became afflicted with osteomalacia, a softening of the bones. They battled rheumatic pain in their limbs, spine, thorax, and pelvic regions, and suffered pervasive general weakness. Children who labored in sweat shops or lived in an urban sprawl under sun-dimming smoke belched out by factories developed rickets.

All these conditions were caused by a severe deficiency of vitamin D. The skin produces vitamin D upon exposure to sunlight. Science solved that particular problem by putting vitamin D in milk. Rickets is all but unknown today.

Living under artificial lighting can be harmful to health. Fortunately, there is a manmade light source that mimics the Sun. All the electric fixtures in my office and home, even the spotlights around the grounds, are fitted with Luxor full-spectrum lights. These lights are the closest manmade source we have to sunlight. They are very beneficial to health.

You might want to consider Luxor's manmade sunlight for your home or workplace. The benefits are very real. I even carry a 185-watt Duro-Test Luxor light globe in my bag when I travel. I am writing this paragraph in the Sheraton Hotel in New Port Richey, Florida, under the light given off by my "traveling sunlight" bulb by Luxor.

There's considerable research that concludes we are born with an internal biological clock. Our internal time clock is set in accordance with the natural dawn-to-dusk light cycles that occur every twenty-four hours. The more nearly we adapt our lifestyle to correspond with our biological clock, the healthier we will be. If we rise at dawn and are active during the daylight hours, the more beneficial our waking hours will be and the more beneficial our dark hours of rest and sleep will be.

If you doubt these conclusions, consider jet lag. High-speed transportation to faraway climes throws our internal time clock out of sync. Jet lag occurs when our biological clock is at odds with the dawn-to-dusk light cycles prevailing at our destination.

Apiarians should try to discipline themselves to awaken each morning sometime between 4:00 and 6:00, depending on the arrival of dawn. If 5:00 is targeted as your year-round time of awakening, your internal time clock will become attuned to it and you will automatically awaken at 5:00.

MY MORNING ROUTINE

I usually awaken naturally each morning around 5:00. I don't use an alarm clock. I don't think it's healthy to be jolted awake artificially by a harsh noise when the body isn't ready to rise. If you don't wake up eager to get going, you probably haven't had enough sleep.

Immediately upon awakening, I take my temperature. After voiding my urine, I weigh myself. At five feet nine inches tall, I allow my weight to fluctuate between 119 and 129 pounds. If my weight rises to 130 pounds or more, I go on a two-day water fast and lose about 4 or 5 pounds, then resume my regular eating habits.

You might think I'm underweight. If you do, you're wrong. In fact, I did not always allow myself to weigh this much. For many years, I kept my weight between 105 and 109 pounds. However, my wife nagged me about my skinny appearance. I made a deal with her that I would gain 10 pounds if she would stop fussing at me to eat more. I gained that 10 pounds at her request. I now maintain this higher weight level in accordance with her wishes. Peace reigns at home.

I believe the American custom of eating three heavy meals every day is a quick ticket to the morgue. For many years, I have been eating three very small meals every day. My body resists both losing weight and putting it on. The way our bodies process food is a perfect example of how magnificently we are constructed.

As I write this chapter, I am experimenting with eating only breakfast in the morning and a combined lunch-dinner between 2:00 and 3:30 in the afternoon. I have been following this routine for eight weeks and have not lost one pound. Does this mean I have been eating too much and too often all these years? It sure looks as if taking only two meals per day can be declared the perfect diet pattern for the apiarian! So be it.

Weight and Health

The less you eat, on average, the healthier you're going to be. It was the Duchess of Windsor who said, "You can't be too rich or too thin." Science has confirmed the back half of that statement.

Studies have shown that consuming fewer calories and maintaining a lean body help extend the life span. There is considerable research in the medical literature that concludes the less you eat, the longer you will live.

In experiments, fish that "fasted" every other day (they were fed only every other day) lived twice as long as the controls, who were fed daily. Other lab animals (rats and mice) given low-calorie, low-volume diets enjoyed increased longevity of 90 to 120 percent over animals given the usual rat or mice chow. A medical doctor at the University of California–Los Angeles Medical School fasts two days per week. He confidently expects this regimen will lengthen his life span. Members of some religious orders routinely fast for varying periods of time.

I believe the best way to manage your weight for optimum health is to gradually reduce your food intake to the point where you experience a very slow, natural weight loss. When you've reached your ideal weight, slightly increase your food intake to maintain lean body-weight equilibrium. You can probably safely assume that your nutrient intake at this point represents your ideal food intake for a lifelong weight-management program for optimum health.

The best time to correct a weight gain is with that first pound over the acceptable maximum. If you weigh yourself daily, as I do, it's easy to modify your lifestyle to eliminate unwanted pounds.

Immediately after my daily weigh-in, I record my weight and body temperature in a ledger I keep handy. After recording these readings, I drink thirty-two ounces of room-temperature Bee-Dew Water (see page 177 for the recipe). Within one minute of ingesting this charged water, peristalsis begins. Drinking down a quart of liquid usually triggers the colonic valve, insuring a healthy and complete emptying of the bowels.

Skin Brushing

Next, I dry-brush massage my face, scalp, and body, going twice over every body part. Dry brushing the skin is an old Scandinavian practice. Although we don't usually think of our skin as an organ, it is. Your skin is a vital, self-cleansing mechanism that does a lot more than just clothe your body. It acts as a barrier to harmful bacteria and helps regulate your internal temperature. It absorbs nutrients, produces vitamin D on exposure to sunlight—and excretes toxins. As much as one third of all the impurities and toxins leaving your body are excreted through your skin, exiting via your pores. More than one pound of metabolic waste is discharged by this complex eliminative organ every day. Chemical analysis confirms that the constituents of sweat are almost identical to those of urine.

When your pores are clogged with millions of dead cells, metabolic wastes and toxic impurities are trapped. Dry-brush massage sweeps away the dry, dead cells on the surface of the skin. This process not only opens the way for the release of impurities, but the tiny capillaries carrying blood to the surface of your body are energized and your entire circulatory system is stimulated. Dry brushing your body makes you feel better all over and gives your skin a healthy glow.

My Personal Recipes

Here are my personal recipes for Bee-Dew Water and Breakfast Bacillus. I hope you will take the time to prepare these electrically charged and fortified elixirs that I have found so beneficial.

Bee-Dew Water

1 teaspoon Bee-Dew Concentrate (see below)
1 teaspoon bee-pollen liquid extract
1 D Cell (see page 178)
1 gallon pure water

1. *Put the Bee-Dew Concentrate and bee-pollen extract in a clean gallon jug.*

2. *Put a funnel in the mouth of the jug. Place the D Cell in the funnel.*

3. *Add the water. (To be certain of absolutely pure water with no additives or contaminants of any kind, I use water from a well over 650 feet deep. You may wish to use water purified by reverse osmosis. To understand why I believe the reverse-osmosis purification method is the best, please see page 163.) Pour the water over the D Cell and let it mingle with the concentrate and extract.*

This is the Bee-Dew Water I drink every morning. Once your body becomes accustomed to the early morning ingestion of this specially prepared drink, you will experience a healthy and speedy evacuation of the intestines and lower colon upon downing the charged mixture. The healthy effects of this regimen will become apparent in short order.

Bee-Dew Concentrate is a catalyst that synergistically boosts the effects of whatever it is combined with. The formula for the concentrate is secret, but the concentrate is an important part of the Bee-Dew Water recipe. See the Source List, page 201, for mail-order sources for this proprietary formula.

Part of the reason this drink is so effective is the D Cell over which the water is poured. No, a D Cell doesn't look like a flashlight battery. It looks like an inch-square chunk of ordinary concrete. But the material is treated by a secret process that enables the cell to capture solar energy. Any liquid poured over a D Cell becomes supercharged because it absorbs some of the Sun's own energy. Plants fed D Cell-charged water grow faster, larger, and healthier than plants given ordinary water. These plants are more productive, too.

About ten or fifteen years ago, I purchased a large number of D Cells from the inventor, a licensed pharmacist. I have enough D Cells on hand to last me and my family until the millennium. To purchase your own supply of D Cells, see the Source List.

Breakfast Bacillus

28 ounces raw, unprocessed honey
4 $\frac{1}{2}$ gallons raw, unpasteurized,
unhomogenized goat's milk
14 ounces Eugalan Topfter
1 pint Continental Acidophilus Bacillus
6 heaping tablespoons Mt. Capra dairy whex

1. *Put the jar holding the honey in a hot-water bath. While you complete steps 2 and 3, the honey will warm. Allow the honey to reach a temperature of about 100°F. It should feel slightly warmer than body temperature.*

2. *Blend the goat's milk with the Eugalan Topfter. Because the Eugalan Topfter powder tends to cake, pour a cup of the goat's milk into a blender, add about one-third of the box of Eugalan Topfter, then blend thoroughly and pour the mixture into a large stainless-steel pan. Repeat this procedure until the entire box of powder has been added to the pan and blended into the milk. Stir thoroughly.*

3. *Add the Continental Acidophilus Bacillus to the goat's-milk mixture. Stir thoroughly.*

4. *Remove the honey from its hot-water bath. By now, it should be well liquified and easy to blend. Add it to the goat's-milk mixture and stir thoroughly.*

5. *Cover the pan. Let the mixture sit undisturbed until it clabbers (curdles) and the cream forms a solid crust on the top. At room temperature, clabbering should occur in thirty-six to forty-eight hours. In the summer, the process can be hurried by placing the pan in the sun. In the hot Arizona sun, clabbering usually takes place in twenty-four to thirty-six hours.*

6. *When clabbering has occurred, break the crust with a spoon and reincorporate it into the mixture. Scoop the crusty pieces into a blender along with some of the liquid and blend for three to four seconds to mix thoroughly. Reincorporate the "crusty" mixture into the smooth mixture.*

7. *Prepare six half-gallon goat's-milk containers. In each one, put 1 heaping tablespoon of dairy whex, then add about one-sixth of the clabbered milk. Leave sufficient head room (about four inches) for the mixture to continue fermenting. Once the containers are filled, shake them thoroughly to blend in the dairy whex. The Breakfast Bacillus is now ready for consumption.*

8. *Place the filled containers in the refrigerator but do not cover them. The very powerful mixture they contain will continue to ferment. If you cap the bottles, gases will pop the tops and the mixture will overflow.*

   Check the bottles occasionally. If the mixture is threatening to rise over the top of a bottle, shake the bottle to calm the mixture down, then decant part of the liquid into another container.

9. *To use the Breakfast Bacillus, remove a bottle from the refrigerator. Give it a good shake to redistribute the honey and blend all the ingredients.*

As I already explained, I drink a serving of Breakfast Bacillus every morning. I pour off 1 pint from my store in the refrigerator and add to it 2 raw fertile eggs, beaten; 2 heaping tablespoons fresh raw bee-pollen granules; 2 heaping tablespoons lecithin granules; 3 squirts propolis extract (or 6 crushed 500-milligram propolis tablets); and 1 tablespoon BioSan Flax Seed Oil. Warm the mixture to body temperature by immersing the container in a hot-water bath. When it's the correct temperature, shake it vigorously. Then enjoy your Breakfast Bacillus feast.

Don't forget to "chew" this liquid powerhouse of nutrients. Take one mouthful at a time. Swish it around in your mouth. "Chew" it eleven times before swallowing it to insure that the digestive enzymes present in your saliva are thoroughly incorporated in the drink.

The ingestion of Breakfast Bacillus following a drink of Bee-Dew Water will cause your digestive tract to become reinhabited with friendly bacteria. When your gastrointestinal tract is colonized with friendly acidophilus bacteria, your entire digestive system will function perfectly.

For my morning dry-brush massage, I use a fabric brush, a rubber pronged plate, and a rough loofah glove. I brush from the top of my head to the tips of my toes. Am I beginning to sound a bit weird? I assure you, I am not. On analyzing the discarded skin cells that sloughed off during a skin conditioning of this type, Dr. Bernard Jensen found they contained nearly 100 percent uric acid. It's nice to know dry brushing rids my body of this toxic substance.

Dry brushing compensates for the wearing of clothes. Because the skin is the largest organ of the body, and the one that absorbs the life-giving nutrients and excretes the toxins, it is beneficial to keep the skin in good working order.

Immediately after my stimulating dry-brush massage, I shave. After shaving, I prepare my Bee-Dew Water for the following morning.

Breakfast Bacillus

In addition to preparing my Bee-Dew Water, I also start getting my breakfast ready. I don't "eat" it yet, but I start "getting it on the table." First, from the refrigerator, I take out sixteen ounces of my previously prepared clabbered, fortified goat's milk, which I call Breakfast Bacillus (see page 178 for the recipe). To this mixture, I add two heaping tablespoons of bee pollen, two heaping tablespoons of crushed lecithin granules, two raw fertile eggs, three squirts of propolis extract (or six crushed 500-milligram propolis tablets), and one tablespoon of flax seed oil. I pop the top on the goat's-milk container and shake everything thoroughly.

Then I draw sufficient hot water to fill the bathroom washbowl and put the container of fortified goat's milk in. The hot water will gradually warm the mixture to body temperature (98°F), which is the ideal temperature for ingesting anything and everything. My Breakfast Bacillus will be warmed and waiting for me when I finish my daily exercises.

I follow the same general routine I just outlined every morning, but I vary my exercise regimen according to the day of the week. I think I already mentioned that, like most people, I find exercise boring. However, I like the remarkable results I derive from it. That's why I built enough variety into my regimen to keep me interested.

MY DAILY EXERCISE PROGRAM

Now I'm ready for the day's exercise. On Monday, Wednesday, and Friday, my exercise of choice is running. On Tuesday and Thursday, I lift weights. Between the two, and all the other accompanying exercises I do, I give myself a very good physical workout every week.

Monday, Wednesday, and Friday

As I just said, on Monday, Wednesday, and Friday, I run. After suiting up, I go outside and spend about fifteen minutes doing

*On Monday, Wednesday,
and Friday, running
is the focal point of
my exercise regimen.*

yoga warm-up exercises. I do alternate toe touches 100 times, run in place for five minutes, and skip rope as fast as I can with both feet together for three minutes.

After my warm-up, I'm ready for my hour's run. I proceed to the road in front of my house prepared to run from eleven to fifteen laps, depending on the season, how I feel that day, and how early I awakened. I engage my stopwatch, set the controls of my exercise computer to monitor my heartbeat, and set off. I run at a pace that keeps my heart at 170 or more beats per minute during my entire run. Every Monday, Wednesday, and Friday, I run as fast as I can for one full hour.

Once in a great while, I don't get to bed until midnight or even later. On these rare occasions, I may not awaken at my usual time of 4:00 to 5:00 A.M. but may sleep to 6:00 or even 7:00. When that happens, I may only run four laps of my regular run. I tell you this to demonstrate that even the best routines should occasionally be sensibly adjusted to circumstances. However, no matter what, I never run less than four laps, which time out to approximately twenty minutes. According to many authorities, at least twenty minutes of continuous running is required for the cardiovascular system to benefit.

No matter how many laps I run on any given day, I pace myself to achieve a heart rate of 170 or more beats per minute throughout my run. During the first half of my last lap, I step up the pace to achieve a heart rate of 180 beats or more. During the last half, I run full-out in an attempt to force my heartbeat to 200 during what is approximately a two-and-a-half-minute period.

All during my run, I always try to beat my personal "world record" time. Unless I compete with myself this way, running becomes so boring that the temptation to quit is very real. Constantly trying to beat my previous time is what keeps me alert and eliminates the boredom.

By the time I hit the finish line, I am perspiring profusely. In spring, summer, and fall, my running shorts and socks are soaking wet. Summer temperatures in Phoenix often top out at over 110°F. Even with our blessed dry air, that's scorching hot. During the hottest days of summer, I have trouble seeing because of the perspiration running down my face and trickling into my eyes. I have to wear a sweatband to keep the droplets out of my eyes.

After finishing my run, I walk down the hill behind my house to my backswing. The backswing is designed to counteract the constant downward pull of gravity by upending the body and reversing the field. I fasten myself to the device and invert my body, ending up head down and feet up in the air. I stay in this upside-down position for one minute. At the end of a minute, I right myself, with my head skyward and feet to the ground. I count off seven seconds in the upright position, then upend myself again.

I invert myself on the backswing eleven times, staying up-

*My backswing is an
important part of
my exercise routine
three days a week.*

side-down about fifty-three seconds out of each minute, upright about seven seconds. This repeated inversion and right-
ing forces the blood to my head and extremities eleven different
times. I developed this backswing routine under the guidance
of Dr. Paavo Airola, the dean of American health writers.

The good, clean, pure, healthy red blood cells cruising
through my veins and arteries after running for an hour comprise the best, most dynamic blood flow I'll experience all day.
When I'm inverted, this hemoglobin-rich, oxygenated blood is
forced to my brain, eyes, head, stomach, heart, and all vital
organs of my body, purifying, cleansing, healing, and repairing
tissues as it goes along.

After eleven minutes of inversion therapy, I hang for five minutes with the aid of a special device designed to help remove the kinks from, stretch, and elongate the spine and limber up the neck. After spending five minutes on this routine, I take my shower.

Because soap destroys the necessary acid mantle of the skin, I wash with water only. I use soap just once a month, on my birth date, the twenty-sixth. Washing the face and body with soap or commercial skin cleansers is counterproductive. Alkaline soap removes the naturally occurring skin oils and protective skin secretions. Besides, the dry-brush massage to which I treat myself every day removes the dead cells and toxins that accumulate on the surface of the skin.

Once my body is completely sluiced off, I turn on the water, make it as hot as I can stand it for a count of eleven, then turn it cold for another count of eleven. I alternate between hot and cold three times, ending with a cold spritz. I owe thanks to Dr. Bernard Jensen for teaching me this invigorating routine.

Tuesday and Thursday

My exercise program on Tuesday and Thursday consists of lifting weights for an hour, concentrating on my back muscles. Thanks to the late, great Bob Hoffman, founder of the York Barbell Company of Pennsylvania, I no longer try to lift heavy weights to my maximum ability. Great strength is not necessary for my lifestyle. I don't believe overtraining and developing bulging muscles is healthy. This effect would add nothing to the quality of my life. Therefore, I now lift lighter weights and do more repetitions. My aim is merely to perspire freely and keep the muscles of my back toned and in good shape. I don't want to carry an excess *ounce* of fat or muscle, let alone a *pound*!

Each extra pound of flesh is equipped with veins and capillaries. The heart has to service those additional passageways. Experts have determined that each pound of excess body weight a person carries—fat or muscle—forces the heart to pump the entire blood supply an extra mile every year. If you're hauling around an extra five pounds, your heart has to labor to service an extra five miles of passageways annually. You never see overweight people of 100 or 125 years of age. Think about it. Excess body fat is a killer.

To do my back exercises, I place a bar across my shoulders. I extend my arms and clasp each end of the bar, bend over, and alternately touch my left and right toes 101 times. I do four sets of 101 toe touches.

I also do 42 chins on my chinning bar. I used to think my chinning ability was extraordinary for my age group. Then I discovered the world record for a man in his seventies is 155 chins. I no longer talk about my chinning accomplishments.

I have been lifting weights for at least 25 years. Consequently, I know how my body reacts to this type of exercise. I find I can miss chinning or working out with weights for as long as a week and still pick up where I left off, still do the maximum reps and chins I did the week before. But, if I miss ten days, I can feel my strength receding. The longer the time is between workouts, the greater is the loss of strength.

If you want to develop your strength and muscles in a hurry, you should lift weights, targeting each muscle group, every other day. If you want to tone and condition your muscles and slowly increase your strength, you should lift weights twice a week.

After completing my weekday exercises, I shower and prepare for breakfast.

MY BREAKFAST

By the time I'm ready to sit down and enjoy my breakfast, I've already put in what to many people would be a full day of activity. I've exercised, showered, dry brushed my skin, and cleansed my colon. My breakfast is what helps give me the energy to go through the rest of my day. The experts say breakfast is the most important meal of the day. It's a very important part of my daily routine.

To start, I check my ledger for what my body temperature registered that morning. Broda Barnes, M.D., informed me his lifelong research on the action of the thyroid gland convinced him that 98°F is the ideal body temperature. When body temperature falls below 98°, Dr. Barnes says the thyroid needs a nudge.

Nudging the thyroid is a matter of individual judgment. My method is to take one grain of desiccated thyroid with my Breakfast Bacillus if my morning temperature is below 98°F. If my temperature registers between 97.0° and 97.5°, I take two grains of desiccated thyroid. If my temperature is exactly 98.0° or higher, I take no thyroid.

After checking my ledger and getting out my dose of thyroid tablets, I'm ready for my Breakfast Bacillus, my "doctored" goat's milk. By now, it's been nicely warmed to body temperature in its hot-water bath. If I am taking thyroid that morning, I chew the tablet well, then take a large mouthful of the goat's-milk mixture, swishing it throughout my mouth before swallowing. This is tantamount to chewing and insures complete digestion and assimilation.

At this time, I also take three 400-I.U. vitamin-E capsules, as formulated by Betty Lee Morales. The Betty Lee Brand formula is a concentrated mixture of all eight natural tocopherols. I burst the caps with my teeth and chew until I am certain all the E oil has been expelled. I spit out the gelatin caps.

I take vitamin E on a regular basis. Health authorities say this is a good way to elevate the healthy high-density lipoproteins (HDLs) and lower the harmful low-density lipoproteins (LDLs). Studies show the total content of serum cholesterol in the bloodstream is not the best indicator of heart-attack risk. It's far more important to have the correct ratio of HDL to LDL. If your HDL count is twice as much as your LDL level, there's little risk of arteriosclerotic-plaque buildup. Researchers at the University of Oregon have found it is unlikely someone with HDL levels of 75 or greater will ever develop heart disease, provided their LDL levels are kept under control.

This, then, is my breakfast. It may not appeal to everyone, but it sure does the trick for me.

GIVE US THIS DAY OUR DAILY BEE PRODUCTS

By now you certainly know that I consider the products of the

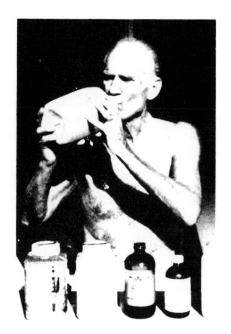

*I drink what I call
Breakfast Bacillus—
goat's milk fortified with
beehive products—every
morning except Sunday.*

beehive to be the best foods in this tired, old world. Because I insist
on organically grown, vine- or tree-ripened fruits and vegetables, my
menus necessarily vary with the seasons. For example, in the summer months, I have fresh tree-ripened fruits along with my Breakfast
Bacillus. In winter, when there's not much fresh fruit to be had, I have
goat's-milk cheese with my breakfast drink.

The only constants in my diet are bee pollen, propolis, and
royal jelly. We really are what we eat, folks. These powerful foods
from the beehive are what are keeping me young, active, healthy,
vital, and strong.

About 10:00 or 11:00 in the morning, I munch three or four
bee-pollen tablets or eat a bee-pollen bar, sometimes two. These
bars are such dynamite nutrition, they can ruin my appetite for
the next meal. I guess that's one reason they work so well in a
weight-loss program. I know from personal experience why
President Reagan calls these bars meal replacements. They
really do the job.

In the summer, except on Sunday, my lunch and dinner do
not vary much. Between noon and 1:00 P.M., depending on my

work flow, I have lunch. During the summer, which begins with a vengeance in Arizona around the beginning of May and lasts until about the beginning of October, I eat fruit with a handful of raw bee-pollen granules. I usually take one heaping teaspoonful of bee pollen along with a juicy bite of fruit and chew these two natural foods together, masticating well for good digestion.

I try to eat only organically grown, in-season fruits. Ideally, the fruits will have ripened on the vine or tree. During the course of the summer, I eat a variety of fruits, everything from mangoes to grapes. Generally speaking, however, when mangoes are in season and the taste is best, I eat mangoes to the exclusion of all other fruits. Not only do I think mangoes have the best taste, I believe that they are the most healthy of all the fruits.

My next fruit choice is watermelon, closely followed by peaches and pears from Arizona and Colorado. I often enjoy a salad of fresh greens with an all-natural poppyseed-and-honey dressing. In season, I eat raw corn-on-the-cob. Yes, raw. It is a pleasure to nibble off those sweet kernels bursting with sun-warmed juices.

For an afternoon snack, usually around 2:30 to 3:30, I eat two to five bee-pollen tablets. If I am planning on skipping dinner, I may munch several bee-pollen lunch bars. I really don't have a set afternoon snack. I operate more on impulse.

For both lunch and dinner, I consume between sixteen and twenty ounces of freshly juiced vegetables. About half of the juice is fresh carrot juice. The other half is made from a mixture of fresh greens and other vegetables in season. Celery juice is a favorite addition.

Get ready for a shocker. During the winter months, I used to eat four to six ounces of raw liver for lunch and dinner every day. Now I take my raw liver only once. I try to eat only the most valuable foods, in their most natural form, from each food group. I rationalize that the big cats, the carnivores, instinctively know more about nutrition than modern man does. When one of Nature's meat-eaters brings down its prey, it eats the choicest bit—the liver—first (see page 156). Because I believe commercial meat producers have less time to bastardize the liver of calves than that of mature animals, I always eat the liver of very young, organically raised vealers.

However, I don't recommend everyone eat raw meat. The experts strongly warn that raw meat may contain harmful bacteria, which are destroyed by the heat of cooking. I have demonstrated to my personal satisfaction that my high intake of the products of the beehive protects me from injurious bacteria. Over the years, my body has become accustomed to eating raw foods, including raw liver.

If you want to put this power protein on your own menu, I suggest that you take desiccated liver in powdered or capsule form.

I believe one of the greatest nutritional sins in the world regularly committed by man is the eating of cooked foods, especially cooked proteins. Sooner or later, the American consumer must realize that the primary cause of many of the degenerative diseases plaguing this great land is the consumption of foodstuffs that have had their original nutrients either cooked away or processed out.

Another nutritional mistake we make in the United States is our heavy consumption of fat-loaded foods. It isn't only that we eat too much red meat, you know. We also consume too much dairy, including pasteurized and homogenized cow's milk, butter, ice cream, and cheese.

Apiarians eat a healthy variety of natural whole foods, preferably raw, along with those storehouses of live nutrients, the products of the beehive.

MY EVENING ROUTINE

I normally work a very full day. I seldom leave my office until around 8:00 in the evening. Upon arriving home, I retreat to the sanctuary of my bathroom. There I exercise my gums, put mineral oil in my ears, pull on my swimming trunks, and go to my backyard swimming pool.

I usually swim fifty laps in my pool, which is fifty feet long. I don't know why I don't swim fifty-three laps, which would total one mile, but I never do. After my swim, I strap on a twenty-

With my twenty-pound belt and snorkel equipment, I'm ready to climb into my heated therapy pool.

pound belt, put on my snorkel equipment, and climb into my therapy pool. Although my swimming pool is never heated, my therapy pool is always kept at 110°F. Breathing through my snorkel, I stay completely submerged for seven minutes with the aid of my twenty-pound belt, climb out, remove my snorkel and belt, swim a quick lap in my unheated swimming pool, then put on my equipment again and return to the 110° therapy pool for another seven minutes. I repeat this procedure three times.

My water therapy and swimming routine was designed by Paul Bragg. Paul Bragg was an early crusader in the health-food movement and is a strong advocate of the natural way of life.

After this invigorating regimen, I return to my house, take a shower, go in my den, and read the evening paper. By this time, it's about 11:00 and I retire. I sleep soundly and awaken naturally between 4:00 and 6:00 the following morning.

MY WEEKEND ROUTINE

Saturday is not exactly a day of rest and relaxation for me. Although I don't exercise or work out, I follow my usual wake-up routine before going to the office. I enjoy the same menu as the day before and return home around dusk. If you're getting the idea that my business affairs keep me very busy— perhaps too busy—you're right!

The Sabbath, however, is a day of rest and of worship. My family is Episcopalian and attends St. Barnabas of the Desert in Paradise Valley, Arizona. After worship, we often breakfast with friends at the Camelback Inn Country Club in summer, the Hilton Hotel in winter. My breakfast consists of whatever fresh fruits are on the menu. I know I would be better off with raw goat's milk, but no restaurant on this planet—at least none I know about—offers it.

It's not possible for dedicated apiarians to dine out properly. I travel considerably. My business takes me to many places, both in the United States and around the world. For example, I am writing this particular section in New York, at the Sheraton Inn, the night before the New York City Marathon.

Without a doubt, a lot of business socializing takes place over meals. The working lunch, dinner, even breakfast, are accepted parts of the workaday world. Sometimes, I must partake. Many restaurants now offer selected packets of herbal teas. It's always possible to order an "undressed" green salad (my favorite is spinach) or a vegetable plate. Of course, I always carry a supply of beehive products. Although I don't fly on Air Force One, my travel rations always include a box or two of President's Lunch Bars and raw bee-pollen granules. I know for a fact Ronald Reagan made sure he had a supply of both of these on his many presidential trips. I also carry bee-pollen tablets, bee-pollen capsules, propolis, and twenty-four-hour royal jelly.

MY QUARTERLY ROUTINE

I closely monitor my body every day without thinking too much about it. I've been doing it for so long now that I can usually tell approximately what my internal chemical balance is just by the way I feel.

Still, forewarned is forearmed. For this reason, I have a hair analysis done quarterly to make sure the mineral levels in my body are in appropriate balance. Because I eat clean food and drink very pure water, I almost never have an excess of any particular mineral in my body.

However, I have occasionally been low in some trace element. When this occurs, I simply step up my intake of bee pollen for ninety days. By then, another quarterly analysis is due. If that analysis shows all minerals are once again in healthy balance, I revert back to my usual daily intake of bee pollen to maintain the optimum levels.

I also have a blood test done quarterly. I instruct the lab technician to read not only my total cholesterol but also my HDL and LDL levels. My normal cholesterol reads between 110 and 134. My triglycerides usually fall between 50 and 65.

I personally monitor my resting heartbeat every morning. My heart usually beats about forty to forty-five times per minute. I occasionally take my own blood pressure. Generally, it is about 120 over 60. These measurements are considered too low by orthodox medical practitioners. Still, I believe they are nearly perfect for apiarians who are careful about their diet and exercise regularly.

Before giving you general guidelines on your internal readings, I want to tell you of an experience I had at the Nevada Clinic for Preventive Medicine in Las Vegas. Dr. Betty Lee Morales told me about the Nevada Clinic and suggested I go through the diagnostic procedures. I did. At the close of the tests, Dr. F. Fuller Royal, the director, said my readings were all "so low" that he believed I had leukemia. Either I had leukemia, he said, or something had gone haywire with the calibration of their diagnostic instruments and he would have to call in experts to reprogram all the paraphernalia.

Dr. Royal explained there was only one type of electronic microscope powerful enough to detect cancer cells in the bloodstream. This microscope was in the laboratory of Arnold Schenk, a medical doctor working in Tijuana, Mexico. Dr. Royal urged me to go see Dr. Schenk.

I wasn't worried, mind you. I knew I did not have leukemia. I knew my Apiarian Lifestyle was keeping me well protected. But I was curious. I made the trip to Mexico to Dr. Schenk's facility. He drew blood, made a slide, then examined the blood specimen closely under his powerful electronic microscope. There were no cancerous cells hitching a ride in my blood.

When Dr. Royal was informed of the results, he acknowledged that his instrument readings were accurate and admitted he was going to have to change his thinking, not recalibrate his equipment. He even went so far as to acknowledge that the so-called average levels may actually be a bit on the high side.

From my personal observations, I have concluded that apiarians in good health will generally exhibit the following readings:

- Blood cholesterol: 110–135
- High-density lipoproteins: 75–100 (or higher)
- Triglycerides: 55–65
- Resting heart rate: 35–45
- Blood pressure: 120 over 60

Keep in mind, however, that I am not a medical doctor and that these guidelines are based purely on my own experiences.

COMMITTING TO APIARIANISM

Once you've committed yourself to the Apiarian Lifestyle, you've taken an enormous first step toward improved health and well-being. No one knows better than I that a lot of self-discipline is required to make such enormous changes in diet and lifestyle.

I hope, however, that this book will give you the necessary nudge toward commitment and follow-through. The Apiarian Lifestyle works, folks. You'll feel better. You'll look better. You'll live longer. You'll enjoy a higher quality of life. Science confirms it. I personally guarantee it.

Conclusion

I am convinced my high ingestion of the products of the beehive plus my vigorous lifestyle play the primary role in keeping me young, healthy, and active in my mid-70s. I am equally convinced every cell in my body continues to regenerate. Because science says the entire body is renewed one cell at a time over a period of 7 years, I fully expect to be brand new and going strong at age 110. I'm not getting older, you see. I'm getting better.

The American Cancer Society says we can cut cancer fatalities in half by the year 2000. The American Heart Association says we can similarly reduce the shocking incidence of heart attacks. Both these prestigious organizations, as well as the United States government, have published diet (and lifestyle) guidelines designed to accomplish these goals.

Every health authority in the universe (finally) concedes diet and lifestyle play a major role in keeping us well—or making us sick.

You control every bite of food you put in your mouth. You decide whether to sit and sag or get up and get going. Health-care practitioners in every specialty you can name agree the diet and lifestyle factors known to foster aging can be inhibited. You have control of the major factors involved. You don't have to settle for a sick and sorry old age. You can stay healthy, active, and attractive well beyond the Biblical limit of three-score years and ten. I have passed that milestone and I'm still going strong. I know the Apiarian Lifestyle will do it for you, too.

You control your diet. You decide your lifestyle. However, if you really want to improve your health and extend your life span, you almost certainly need to make some big changes in your lifestyle.

If you need an incentive to make the necessary changes, give some thought to how much longer and how much healthier you want to live. Do you want to live twenty more years? Fifty more years? In what condition?

The quality of life you enjoy is more important than your biological age. I have known youngsters of twenty-five who were worn out and apathetic. I have known grand oldsters of ninety-five who greeted each day with eagerness and boundless energy.

You decide.

In Chapter 8, I told you how I have achieved optimum health by living the Apiarian Lifestyle. I am thriving on it and am sure you would, too. But, realistically, I know most people won't summon up the will power needed to follow it every day in every way for the rest of their lives.

Even so, you probably have a pretty good idea of the changes you need to make in your diet and lifestyle in order to achieve optimum health and then sustain it for the whole of your extended life span. I'm convinced you can enjoy *better* health— yes, *super* health or even *perfect* health—if you have the determination and self-discipline necessary to eat and drink only what is best for you, to do what is best for you. When you think about it, to give yourself less than the best is almost suicidal.

I believe the single most important change you can make in your diet is to put the products of the beehive on your menu every single day. This entire book is well and truly—medically and scientifically—documented. I've given you a plethora of solid facts showing the many benefits all the bees' gifts offer. The importance of bee pollen, propolis, royal jelly, and honey in human nutrition has been established beyond doubt.

To make it easier for you to start living the Apiarian Lifestyle, I have compiled a Source List for you. The list begins on page 201. I've even included two firms that can provide you with beekeeping equipment, plus the bees you need to populate a hive, if you want to "grow your own" products of the beehive.

Beekeeping is one of the most ancient and honored professions on the planet. I'm proud to report I not only head up a company that is probably the largest harvester and producer of beehive products in the world, but I'm also a beekeeper myself. I have my hives tucked away behind my garage. And, yes, I work those hives personally. Once you know what you're doing, tending bee colonies is very relaxing. I enjoy it—a lot.

I carry on extensive correspondence with like-minded individuals all over the world. I would be pleased to hear from any reader who has benefited from the products of the beehive or has comments on this book. You can write to me in care of Avery Publishing Group, 120 Old Broadway, Garden City Park, NY 11040. I know what the Apiarian Lifestyle has done for me. I expect it will do the same for you, even in a modified form, so I am looking forward to a substantial increase in my mail.

It's been a pleasure visiting with you via the printed page. The next time you're buzzed by a bee when you are outdoors, don't forget to say thank you. Without the hard-working honeybee to pollenize the many beautiful flowers and food crops, life as we know it would cease to exist. I offer myself as living proof the Apiarian Lifestyle works. Simply taking advantage of the many benefits the products of the beehive offer can be a giant first step toward better health and extended longevity.

Get started now. Make a list. Jot down the changes you *need* to make in diet and lifestyle, plus those you feel you *can* and *will* make. As you achieve one goal, cross it off and work on the next. Try for perfection. Be persistent. Discipline yourself.

Take that first step. Better health and extended longevity are yours for the doing. You really can improve your health and increase your odds in life's sweepstakes. When is the best time to start living healthy? It doesn't matter how old (or young) you are. *The best time to start is right now.*

To your health, naturally. May you live a thousand years, prosper in perfect health, and enjoy the millennium with me!

Beekeeping is not only my business but my hobby. Note that I protect just my eyes and head around my friends, the bees.

SOURCE LIST

There's nothing more frustrating than not being able to find something you need. To make it easy for you to get more information on the healthy products I cite in this book that can't be purchased at your local health-food store, supermarket, or department store, I have compiled a handy reference list. All these places supply the item or items under which they're listed. Some also sell other items, and some will be happy to send you literature and/or a catalog on their wares. Just phone or write.

BEES AND BEEKEEPING EQUIPMENT

Beekeeping equipment
A. I. Root Company
P.O. Box 706
Medina, OH 44258
(800) 289-7668

Bees and equipment
Dadant and Sons, Inc.
51 South Second Street
Hamilton, IL 62341
(217) 847-3324

Pollen trap
The Plains Corporation
3627 East Indian School Road
Suite 209
Phoenix, AZ 85018
Toll-free: (800) 875-0096
In Arizona: (602) 957-0096

HEALTH AIDS

Backswing
Natural Health Foods and
  Barbell Center
6981 Market Street
Youngstown, OH 44512
(216) 758-0111

D Cells
Joe Dun Sloan
6315 Middleton Street
Huntington Park, CA 90255
(213) 589-4128

Full-spectrum lightbulbs,
 globes, and tubes
Duro-Test Corporation
9 Law Drive
Fairfield, NJ 07004
(800) 289-3876

HEALTH BOOKS

The Cancer Answer, by A. E.
 Carter
The New Miracles of Rebound
 Exercise, by A. E. Carter
New Dimensions
 Distributors
16508 East Laser Drive
Suite 104
Fountain Hills, AZ 85268
Toll-free: (800) 624-7114
In Arizona: (602) 837-8322

The Golden Pollen, by
 Marjorie McCormick
Honeybee Pollen and the New
 You, by Jim Devlin
Mr. Bee Pollen Himself, by Jim
 Devlin
Mr. Bee Pollen, Inc.
P.O. Box 26412
Prescott Valley, AZ 86312
(602) 772-2070

I Found the Fountain of Youth,
 by Noel Johnson
The Living Proof, by Noel
 Johnson
Noel Johnson
1370 Beryl Street
San Diego, CA 92109
(619) 272-6243

HEALTH FOODS

Armour desiccated thyroid
Available by prescription only

Mt. Capra dairy whex
Mt. Capra Cheese
279 Southwest 9th Street
Chehalis, WA 98532
(206) 748-4224

Betty Lee Brand vitamin E
Eden Ranch
Box 370
Topanga, CA 90290
(310) 455-2065

MiVita Minerals mineral water
Nature's
122 South Sirrine Street
Mesa, AZ 85210
(602) 969-7207

MAIL-ORDER SERVICES

C C Pollen Company
3627 East Indian School Road
Suite 209
Phoenix, AZ 85018
Toll-free: (800) 875-0096
In Arizona: (602) 957-0096

National Natural Foods
  Catalog
1451 Main Street
Sarasota, FL 34236
(813) 366-7906

New Dimensions Distributors
16508 East Laser Drive
Suite 104
Fountain Hills, AZ 85268
Toll-free: (800) 624-7114
In Arizona: (602) 837-8322

Natural Lifestyle Supplies
16 Lookout Drive
Asheville, NC 28804
Toll-free: (800) 752-2775
In North Carolina: (704) 254-9606

Smokey Mountains Natural
  Foods
15 Aspen Court
Asheville, NC 28806
Toll-free: (800) 926-0974
In North Carolina: (704) 251-2143

BIBLIOGRAPHY

Aagard, K. Lund. "Propolis, Natural Substance, the Way to Health," paper translated from Danish.

ABC and XYZ. Medina, Ohio: A. I. Root Company, 1980.

"Activity of 10-Hydroxydecenoic Acid From Royal Jelly Against Experimental Leukemia and Ascitic Tumors." *Nature*, vol. 183, May 1959.

Airola, Paavo. *Worldwide Secrets for Staying Young*. Phoenix: Health Plus Publishers, 1982.

Alken, C. E., G. Jonsson, and L. Rohl. "Clinical Trials of Cernilton in Chronic Prostatitis." Heidelberg, Germany: University Clinic, March 1966.

Balch, James F., and Phyllis A. Balch. *Prescription for Nutritional Healing*. Garden City Park, New York: Avery Publishing Group, 1990.

Bergman, Arieh, et al. "Acceleration of Wound Healing by Topical Application of Honey." *American Journal of Surgery*, vol. 145, March 1983.

Borneck, R. "The Products of the Hive." *Informations techniques du Directorat des services veterinaires français*, vol. 60/63, 1977.

Brinkley, Ginny, Linda Goldberg, and Janice Kukar. *Your*

Child's First Journey. Garden City Park, New York: Avery Publishing Group, 1988.

Calcaianu, G., and F. Cozma. "Treatment With Bee Products of the Behaviour Troubles in Young People in the Period of Puberty and Teen-Age." Paper presented at the Apitherapy Second Symposium, Romania, [no date].

Carter, Albert Earl. *The Cancer Answer.* Phoenix: ALM Publishers, 1988.

Carter, Albert Earl. *The New Miracles of Rebound Exercise.* Phoenix: ALM Publishers, 1988.

Chauvin, R. "On the Physiological and Therapeutic Effects of Various Pollen Extracts." *La Revue de Pathologie Generale et de Physiologie Clinique,* no. 687, April 1957.

Delperee, Robert. "The Secrets of the Life of Bees." *Royal Society of Naturalists of Belgium and France,* vol. 44, no. 10, 1961.

Donadieu, Yves. "The Use of Honey in Natural Therapeutics," paper presented at the Apitherapy Second Symposium, Romania, [no date].

Dworkin, Stan, and Floss Dworkin. *The Good Goodies.* Emmaus, Pennsylvania: Rodale Press, 1977.

Erasmus, U. *Fats and Oils: The Complete Guide to Fats and Oils in Health and Nutrition.* Vancouver: Alive Books, 1986.

Filipic, B., and M. Likvar. "Clinical Value of Royal Jelly and Propolis Against Viral Infections," paper translated from Slavic.

Ghisalberti, E. L., P. R. Jefferies, and R. Lanteri. *Potential Drugs From Propolis: Mass Spectometry in Drug Metabolism.* New York: Plenum Press, 1977.

Harvesting Honeybee Pollen—Standard Operating Procedure for High-Desert Bee Pollen's Beekeepers. Scottsdale, Arizona: Plains Corporation, 1983.

Hayes, L. J., and R. A. Baldensnerger. "Bees Sterilize Pollen by Means of a Glandular Secretion That Is Antagonistic to Tumors." *L'Apiculteur haut-chinois,* 1958.

Hernuss, Peter, et al. "Pollen Diet as an Adjunct of Radiation Therapy in Gynecological Carcinomas." Vienna, Austria: University of Vienna, [no date].

Hill, R. *Propolis: The Natural Antibiotic.* Wellingborough, Northamptonshire, England: Thorsons Publishers Limited, 1977.

The Hive and the Honey Bee. Hamilton, Illinois: Dadant and Sons, 1975.

"Honey, Infant Botulism and the Sudden Infant Death Syndrome." Sacramento: California Medical Association, 1980.

Hunter, H. A. *Extend Your Life: The Handbook of Natural Healing A Through Z.* Phoenix: ALM Publishers, 1987.

Inada, T., T. Kitagawa, and M. Miyakawa. "Use of Cernilton in Patients With Prostatic Hypertrophy." *Acta Urologica Japonica,* vol. 13, no. 6, June 1967.

Ioyrish, Naum. *Bees and People.* Moscow: MIR Publishers, [no date].

Jensen, Bernard. *Food Healing for Man.* Escondido, California: Bernard Jensen Publications, 1983.

Johnson, Noel. *A Dud at 70—A Stud at 80—And How to Do It.* Scottsdale, Arizona: Plains Corporation, 1982.

Johnson, Noel. *The Living Proof—I Have Found the Fountain of Youth.* Scottsdale, Arizona: Plains Corporation, 1989.

Killion, Gene. "Move Your Colonies With Care." *The American Bee Journal,* vol. 122, no. 12, December 1982.

Kivalkina, V. P., A. I. Balalykina, and V. I. Piontkovski. "Plasmocitary Response in White Mice Immunized With an Antigen Associated With Propolis," paper translated from Russian.

Kivalkina, V. P., and E. L. Budarkova. "Propolis Impact on the Immunogenesis in the Case of Immunization With Anatoxin," paper translated from Russian.

Lamberti, J. R., and L. G. Cornejo. "Presence of Gamma Globulin in Injectable Royal Jelly and Its Use in Revitalizing Processes," paper translated from Spanish.

Leander, Gosta. "A Memorandum Concerning a Statistical Evaluation of the Results of a Clinical Investigation of Cernilton," paper translated from Swedish.

"Maize Pollen—Biostimulator and Supplementary Protein Source in the Feeding of Poultry." *Zeitschrift für Tierphysiologie, Tiernahrung und Füttermittelkunde*, vol. 39, December 1983.

McCormick, Marjorie. *The Golden Pollen: Nature's Unique Force of Life*, 3rd ed. Prescott Valley, Arizona: Mr. Bee Pollen, Inc., 1984.

Mladenov, S. "Diseases of the Air Passages Treated With Honey." Bulgaria: [no date].

Morales, Betty G. "Energy Galore." *Organic Consumer Report*, July 1980.

Murat, Felix. *The Eternal Natural Healer*. No city: By the author, 1981.

Ohkoshi, M., N. Kawamura, and I. Nagakubo. "Clinical Evaluation of Cernilton Efficacy in the Treatment of Chronic Prostatitis." *Japanese Journal of Clinical Urology*, vol. 21, no. 1, 1967.

Osmanagic, I., D. Biljenski, and N. Mavric. "Therapeutic Effects of Melbrosin in Irradiation Diseases." *Apimondia*, September 1978.

Osmanagic, Izet. "A Clinical Testing of the Effect of Melbrosin on Women Suffering From Climacteric Syndrome." Sarajevo, Yugoslavia: University Clinic for Women, May 1972.

Osmanagic, Izet. "Effects of Melbrosin in Cases of Reduced Sexual Potency." Sarajevo, Yugoslavia: University of Sarajevo, [no date].

Palos, E., Z. Voiculescu, and C. Andrei. "Comparative Studies Concerning Biochemical Characteristics of Beebread as Related to the Pollen Preserved in Honey." Romania: Agronomic Institute, [no date].

Pokrajcic, L., and I. Osmanagic. "The Treatment With Melbrosin of Dysmenorrhea in Adolescence." Sarajevo, Yugoslavia: University Clinic for Women, [no date].

"Pollen Preparations and Their Impact on Immunological Reactions on Test Mice," English-language abstract of a paper read at the International Symposium on Apitherapy, 1974.

Popovici, N., and N. Oita. "Influence of Extracts of Propolis in Mitosis," paper translated from Romanian.

Robinson, William. "Delay in the Appearance of Palpable Mammary Tumors in C3H Mice Following the Ingestion of Pollenized Food." *Journal of the National Cancer Institute*, vol. 9, no. 2, October 1948.

Saenz, A. "Biology, Biochemistry, and the Therapeutic Effects of Royal Jelly in Human Pathology." Paris, France: Pasteur Institute, July 1984.

Salajan and Baltan. "Influence of Maize Pollen on Ovulation: Results of Incubation and Biological Value of Hen Eggs." Romania: [no date].

Scheller, S., J. Tustanowski, and Z. Paradowski. "Comparative Study on the Staphylococcus Sensitivity to Propolis and to Antibiotics," paper translated from Polish.

Schmidt, H. W., "Royal Jelly in Diet, Prophylaxis, and Therapy." Lecture given before the German Medical Association, Leipzig, Germany, October 1956.

Scientific Study for Research of Health Foods and Their Benefits for Mankind—The Honeybee Pollen Story. Scottsdale, Arizona: Plains Corporation, 1988.

Soliman, F. A., and A. Soliman. "The Gonad Stimulating Potency of Date Palm Pollen Grains." *Experientia*, October 1957.

Steiner, Rudolf. *Nine Lectures on Bees*. New York: St. George Publications, 1964.

"A Summary of Clinical Tests Concluded With Bee Pollen and Other Substances." *Naturheilpraxis*, 1977.

U.S. Department of Agriculture. Agriculture Research Service. *Beekeeping in the United States*.

Vechet, L. "Effect of Propolis on Some Species of Microorganisms and Molds," paper translated from Czechoslovakian.

Vorwohl, Günther. "Pollen and Honey." Lecture given at the Apiarist Convention, Sontra, Germany, October 1976.

Walker, Morton. *Honeybee Pollen and Other Products From the Beehive.* Stamford, Connecticut: Freelance Communications, 1984.

Weitgasser, Hans. "Royal Jelly in Dermatological Cosmetics." *Medizinische Kosmetick,* [no date].

INDEX

ABOUT THE AUTHOR

Royden Brown is the founder and president of The CC Pollen Company, the largest harvester of honeybee pollen in the United States. For the past twenty years, he has been gathering together all the world's scientific research and data concerning the products of the bee. As recognition for his philanthropic work and pioneering efforts in the bee-pollen industry, Mr. Brown was knighted by the Sovereign Military and Hospitaler Order of Saint John of Jerusalem, Knights of Malta. An ancient order, the Knights of Malta was established in 1048, during the Crusades.

In his mid-seventies, Mr. Brown is a firm believer in the Apiarian Lifestyle, carrying on an incredibly active schedule of managing a business, conducting research and development, and maintaining a rigorous exercise program that would challenge any twenty-five-year-old. He and his wife, Doris, currently reside in Paradise Valley, Arizona.